MULTIPLE DEFENSES
for
WINNING BASKETBALL

Delmer Harris

DISCARD

Parker Publishing Company, Inc.   West Nyack, N.Y.

PRINTED IN THE UNITED STATES OF AMERICA
ISBN−0-13-604777-7
BC

DEDICATION

I want to dedicate the book to my family and my players.

Also — a special thanks to four coaches who helped by reading and commenting on the book: Les Lane, Eric Geldart, Hilton White, and Rudy D'Amico.

The Purpose of This Book

Defensive basketball has become increasingly complex over the last ten years. Since the advent of the innovative and devastating offensive styles known as the Shuffle and the Swing and Go, coaches have applied themselves to developing a counterbalancing defensive game. It would seem that the key to equalizing the strong offensive attack is not just defense *per se* — it is *multiple defense*. While most teams in the not-too-distant past relied on a singular strong defense over the entire season, there are few successful coaches today who do not take at least three defensive weapons into each game: a man-to-man, a zone and a press.

Falling in line with the present trend toward multiple defense, I believe that a team should be able to play all the previously-mentioned, basic three types. In fact, the wise coach will be able to adjust certain aspects of each of his three standard defenses which will tend to give a very "multiple" complexion to his defensive game. The purpose of the book is fourfold: (1) to explain my ideas about the three basic types of defense, (2) to show adjustments for each in order to present an even more multiple effect, (3) to illustrate drills for teaching purposes, and (4) to advise how one can use multiple defenses strategically in the game situation.

I will not attempt to promote one defensive type above any other. There is *need* to having each defense. Many books have made a good presentation of the man-to-man variations in the past. But it is my feeling that writers have not explained the zones or even the presses nearly so well. Much of this book will be directed toward the zones and presses, hopefully adding to the general understanding of those defenses. The multiple defense system will be explained, plus how to teach and use it without adding too much burden to the teaching task each coach faces.

When I speak of using *multiple defenses* I address the coach at every level. What I recommend is that the coach select a basic way to teach each separate area: the man-to-man, the zone and a press. He must *teach the basics first*. Gradually, he will be able to add one or two of the various manners of adjusting from the basic so that his team ends the season a versatile defensive unit. The teaching load is not as great as one might imagine, since a team would have only three defenses with, say, maybe two or three adjustments rather than six to nine totally different ones. Using carry-over techniques in ruling and teaching, the multiple defense system allows versatility that would otherwise be most difficult. This book does not intend to describe every known way to adjust a defense or to make zone slides or press movements. It will set forth a case for using multiple defenses in ways that have brought success to our teams. The astute coach at any level will be able to apply his own ideas to fit his theories and his needs and to find what he can use in his situation in a particular season as well as what he cannot. It is this mutual sharing of ideas that has made this book possible.

———*Del Harris*

Table of Contents

1

Using the Tools of Multiple Defense Effectively

In the following chapters we have identified some of the many options each coach has to choose from as he selects his defense. In using the multiple defense system it is important to understand our basic point of view. That is, we believe each coach should select one type of half-court defense as his base defense. As the year progresses he should teach his players how to adjust that defense by using over-plays, traps, rules and other simple alterations. The coach should also develop a press defense for use in at least desperation circumstances and preferably as a change of pace during other stages of the game. Last he should install a half-court defense of a contrasting type from the base defense to use as a change of pace at the half-court level. *This is as far as the coach need go to be functional in the multiple defense game.*

Under certain conditions some coaches will want to add to the defensive arsenal and put in more defensive variations. We have done so each year, but if it is not absolutely desirable to broaden the defense, we would say the basic three defensive tools are adequate. The reason we have been able to use more than our share of defenses is that we have stressed the similarity of defensive types. We employ rules and use drills which are pertinent to the moves we are teaching. The core fundamentals we teach as described in chapters 2 and 3 lay a foundation upon which we build our multiple defense system. The zones and the presses are built on this man-to-man base.

If a coach selects the man-to-man as his team's first defense he can adjust it at half-court four distinct ways regarding player positioning: regular, laning, sagging, and trapping. In addition he can overplay individuals or an entire team in a certain direction to become even more multiple. He must drill his players to beat the individual opponent and to handle the fundamental two- and three-man moves as well as to stop team patterns. He will *not* have time to go so deeply into the zone type of defense and will not be able to use the match-up as successfully as the coach who adopts zone as his base defense. But by using the zone rules in chapter 6 and explaining the desired formation and slides that fit his team, he can have his team put up a most adequate change of pace zone defense.

If the coach decides zone defense suits his team's abilities better, he will not be able to develop as tough a team man-to-man defense as the coach who uses this as his best, of course. But by teaching the fundamentals that in our opinion he must begin with to have any good defense, he will have made a good start at developing a man-to-man suitable for changing pace. If he will rule the switches and go over the basic team moves frequently, he can expect reasonable success with the man-to-man.

If zone defense is selected as the main defense, the coach will be able to use many zone adjustments and formations. We believe the zone team should be able to contain, lane, and press with their basic defense. They may gradually learn to match-up with that same defense and might possibly even learn a new formation or two as further change of pace measures.

For example, if a coach selects a 1-2-2 zone as his base defense, he should begin by teaching the basic defensive fundamentals of chapters 2 and 3. He would then teach the zone rules in chapter 6. He would follow this up by teaching the desired containing slides in chapter 7, the laning adjustment in chapter 8 and then, hopefully, the matching style found in chapters 9 and 10. This would give his team a very adjustable zone game.

We believe that teaching the press defenses is an easy matter if a good job has been done at teaching half-court defense. It is mainly a matter of expanding the rules regarding such things as switching and trapping to cover the full court. The methods are the same. That is, a team that can trap at half-court can do so full-court. Lack of speed may limit their effectiveness at full-court but the technique is nearly the same.

There are only two slight differences in trapping full-court instead of half. One, the full-court trap can be set more often because an escape pass does not yield an open shot immediately in most cases. Two, a full-court presser tries to prevent the split first of all while the half-court trapper approaches the ballhandler more in the pass lane to his man to slow the return pass down. The quick return pass is troublesome at half-court since the man left open is usually in scoring range. The rest of the techniques of trapping and rotating are the same at all court levels whether using zone or man-to-man. This allows a lot of versatility in pressing.

We believe the beauty of pressing is in its simplicity. The team that understands the three vertical trap lanes, the four trap slides, plus how and when to rotate can play any zone or man-to-man press by using the same fundamentals. Application of this knowledge has made our teams high-scoring and well-known for their pressing game. Yet we have spent less time working specifically on our press than on any of the major parts of our game.

We facilitate our teaching of the multiple defense game by starting our freshman team right into the system from the beginning. We do not have to start over each year with our players because of this. They use the man-to-man as their base defense but learn to use some zone and how to press full-court. Our varsity may use either man-to-man or zone as the base defense, but regardless they are able to build on the carry-over from their first year. High school coaches are able to begin the teaching process in the junior high and they certainly should. A high school junior-senior team could really become a versatile defensive unit if they were taught the basics of the defensive system in the lower grades. The coach who must start anew each year really limits his team's chances for adjustability.

USING COMBINATION OR ALTERNATING DEFENSES

Aside from the standard defenses we have been advocating, we confess to having employed some of the less-popular and less-used defensive change-up styles. We have resorted to one of these whenever we felt we could not be successful in a standard defense. The following defenses we will describe are not ones that a team would use as a basic defense. But if a team is well-grounded in basic methods of defense, they may be able to use one of these changes even without much practice for a short period in a game with just enough success to give victory. We have won many games by going into one of these more unusual defenses for five or ten minutes. If the opponent hesitates in adjusting to our change and allows us to get a few points ahead during that time, we may be able to nurse that lead into victory. If a team is an underdog and can out-score its opponent by ten points during a specific six or eight minutes, it can lose the rest of the game by eight points and still be the victor. Sometimes a defensive change the opponent has not prepared for will provide this gap. We have found this to be the case frequently.

Many of the old-time coaches look with disdain on playing with defense in such a manner. Regardless of one's personal feelings about this, it is good to know all the possibilities available to a coach. With the better, stronger teams the less playing around a coach does the better off he will be in a vast majority of cases. However, when defeat in imminent, who knows but what an occasional wrinkle might bring about success. We will elaborate somewhat on a few of the moves we have used. Probably each coach can come up with a little variation all his own; we are not attempting to catalog them all.

The Matchbox and One

When an opponent has an unbalanced offensive game, a box and one will occasionally stop the big scorer and throw the team off stride or into panic. Or, by keeping the key playmaker from handling the ball, the defense might get similar results. Occasionally the same is done to stop a fine rebounder. Diagram 1-1 shows the standard box and one moves as the ball goes to the corner. Players 3 and 4 must use the tandem rule. All the box players will

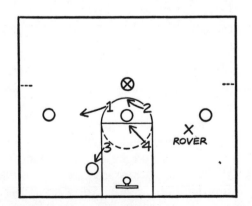

Diagram 1-1

try to match-up as well as possible with the other four offensive players. They try to avoid guarding empty space. One interesting point to consider is to allow the weakest defender to guard in the man-to-man spot as the rover. The reason to try this is that it is more difficult to play smart box defense than it is to stay as close to one man as possible. Besides, the box will help the rover if the star offensive man gets away.

The Triangle and Two

If the opponent has two really outstanding boys, the triangle might work. It is more risky than the matchbox and one. But these defenses are emergency measures anyway. Diagram 1-2 shows the triangle players. If both players being played man-to-man were forwards the triangle would be raised so that the 2-man base was more toward the front positions, particularly until one of the key men got the ball. The basic idea is for 1 to chase the ball out front and try to cover the point area. Players 2 and 3 cover the post and corners. One of them, the one on the ball side, will rise to help the point man whenever the offense begins to hurt the defense out front. The men playing man-to-man must play hard defense, but again, the smarter defenders should be in the zone. It takes a lot of ability to play the triangle effectively.

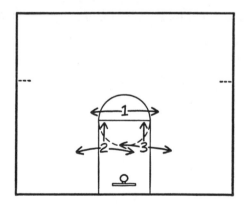

Diagram 1-2

Alternating Defenses

There are any number of ways to alternate defenses. The most basic way has been to use a man-to-man when your team scored and a zone if it failed to do so. Some teams add a press if their team hits a free throw. From there it may flower into a hundred possible combinations. If the coach will keep in mind that he has several defensive possibilities to select from—full-court press (zone or man-to-man), other area presses, half-court zones of all types, half-court man-to-man variations, combination defenses—he can visualize just how complex this alternating can get. Some teams key their changes by whether they score or not their last time down the floor. Others alternate by the scoreboard: they use one defense when the unit's digit is even, another if it is odd. Or they set one defense if their unit digit is from 1-5, another if it is from 6 to 0.

Some coaches have been known to hold up various colored towels, each color indicating the defense to use that time down the floor. Others allow a player to signal with numbers of fingers, or vocally, or by floor position, or arm position the various changes as they are desired. Other ways to alternate defenses are to change from one to another after the ball is thrown in against a press, or when the ball crosses the half line, or whenever a trap is thrown. Some teams will key on which side of the half line the ball is dribbled as it enters the front court. Again, if the ball is worked to the defensive right side first, the defense may use a different type than if it were thrown to the middle or left side.

There are many possibilities to use as keys. While it may seem ridiculous to hear the extremes some have gone to, when one coaches against a team that changes like that he will find it can occasionally give an offense fits for a while. Most games are won or lost in just a few of the game's total minutes. Our thinking in general on these variations is to make sure the other team is more confused than ours is, or get back to something we can do better.

SELECTING THE RIGHT DEFENSE FOR AN OPPONENT

The problem of selecting the best basic defense for one's own team is a complex problem each coach must work out for himself as he weighs his personnel and his own teaching abilities. Less involved is the choice of defensive style to use against a particular opponent. In the following paragraphs we will generalize briefly how a coach might alter defenses for a specific opponent or to change the tempo of a game. The coach must bear in mind that an occasional change in *offensive* style may be more effective in changing the game tempo in a given situation; however, we believe that defensive changes are called for much more often.

Good scouting reports are vital to the coach who plays an adjustable defensive game. Naturally, if he does not change with his defenses, a scouting report is of less consequence. A good report will detail the opponent's pattern, their relative inside and outside power, and individual strengths and weaknesses. We hope to be able to use our best defense to begin a game while adjusting somewhat to the opponent's pluses and minuses. Occasionally, we feel our base defense is just not called for, but not often. That is, even if a team is known to be more effective generally against a man-to-man and our base defense is man-to-man, we will normally challenge them with our best defense to see if they can execute better than we. If we know from previous experience that they can overpower our normal defense, we will try to begin with a change-up defense on them. The point is, use your own strength when possible. But do not whip a dead horse; it can be just as effective to play to the opponent's weakness.

It is important that the coach not get carried away with the idea of defensive changes. *He should make adjustments within the base defense first before abandoning it for another.* A team can change too often as well as not enough. A coach must develop the knack to feel when adjustments cannot turn the tide and a new defense is necessary.

Getting a feel for momentum in a game is an important step for the coach. We try not to change defenses while we have game momentum on our side. On the other hand when we feel the opponent has taken the initiative in a game, we give serious consideration to the possibility of defensive adjustment or change. A possession chart such as is shown in Diagram 1-3 helps give the coach an idea of whether the defense is being effective. In general if the opponent is scoring at the rate of a point per possession of the ball, they are being effective. Unless the coach's team is doing considerably better offensively, a change may be in order. On the sample chart the numbers indicate the player's number who shot the ball or did the item indicated by the abbreviation before the number as the chart indicates. At the start of the game the opponent was doing well against our man-to-man. They had scored 21 points the first 17 possessions. We had only 15 points. We changed to a zone press with about ten minutes remaining and took a 42-37 half-time lead. Having a manager near the coach

POSSESSION CHART

ABBREVIATIONS — RB-Rebound; JB-Jumpball; ST-Steal; DD-Double dribble; TR-Travel; O-Basket made; 3s-Three seconds; F-Foul; etc.

METHOD BALL OBTAINED	FGA–FG	FTA–FT	HOW BALL LOST	TYPE OF OFFENSIVE MOVE	FAST BREAK?	COMMENTS SUCH AS DEFENSIVE CHANGES. ETC.
1 JB	(14)			JB PLAY	✓	BOTH MAN-TO-MAN
2 FG-13			TR-14			
3 FG-13		20	RB-13			
4 ST-14	20-(20)					
5 RB-50	14		RB-51			
6 FT-21	(50)			1st CUTTER		
7 FG-31		(53)				7-7 16:08
8 RB	(40)		RB-51			
9 FG-23			DD-12			
10 FG-23	40				✓	
11 OB on 23	40-(50)					
12 FG-21	20-50		RB-51			
13 RB-14	(20)			SHUFFLE		13-13 13:15
14 FG-23	14-20		RB-51		✓	
15 FT-21-21		20	RB-31			
16 FG-51	(14)					
17 FG-13	30		RB-13			15-21 10:20, OUT TIMEOUT
18 TR-13	(30)					ZONE PRESS
19 RB-30	(14)					
20 DD-15	14-50		RB-55			
21 ST-14	(14)				✓	
22 ST-30	(30)				✓	23-21 8:40 THEIR
23 FG-23	20		RB-55			TIMEOUT
24 ST-20			TR-20			
25 FG-51	30		RB-31			
26 FT-51	(50)			1st CUTTER		
27 RB-50	20				✓	
28 FT-31	(14)				✓	
29 RB-30		(14)(14)				
30 FG-51			TR-20			
31 OF-12	(12)					31-29 5:51 OUT TIMEOUT
32 RB-12	30-50		RB-51			
33 RB-30	(30)			SCREEN-ROLL		
34 FG-31	(30)					
35 FG-21		(50)	RB-31			
36 ST-30		50				
37 TR-21	14-30		RB-55		✓	
38 FG-51	(30)			SHUFFLE		38-35 2:4- THEIR
39 RB-30	20		RB-51			TIMEOUT
40 ST-14	(14)				✓	
41 RB-50			TR-30			
42 FG-13	(30)					42-37 HALF-TIME
43						
44						
45						

Diagram 1-3

during the game who keeps this chart is most helpful in keeping aware of momentum both offensively and defensively.

The following list of suggestions will relate some adjustments and changes that we might possibly use:

1. Against a strong inside team we may use a sagging man-to-man or a containing style of zone. However, we may press instead, trying to force the bigger men out on the floor. We may zone the forwards and man-to-man the guards, or vice-versa.

2. Against a team with good driving guards we will avoid taking many chances pressing them. We will play a more containing or position zone defense at half-court. We may try to over-play heavily on the inside. Or we may use a containing man-to-man defense.

3. Against a team with good outside shooters we may press full-court to hurry them or to influence someone other than the best shooters to take the shots in the event the best shooters are the guards. We may play a forcing man-to-man, a lane zone or even a containing zone that is instructed to push out fast to the good shooters.

4. Against a good fast-breaking and running team we may go to a man-to-man full-court press. The press would be instructed to contain the offense, to slow it down rather than try to trap and steal.

5. Against a young and inexperienced team we might try alternating defenses after a goal or on some other key, figuring they might not adjust well. Or we might press, particularly if their ballhandling is unsure.

6. When our team gets into foul trouble we may change to a containing zone, hoping to avoid fouling.

7. Against a strict pattern team we might press full-court. We might use a lane zone or a laning man-to-man at half-court.

8. Against a team that free lances and drives or punches the ball in well, we would try to play a containing style of defense.

9. Against a team with little movement in their zone offense or whenever a team uses a zone pattern repeatedly we will match-up.

10. Against a team that has our offense stymied we might begin pressing to get our offense started again.

11. Against a team that is scoring well against us we will try to adjust by moving our point of initial pressure or by adjusting any of a number of ways. Or we may go to a change-up defense or a combination defense to shut off a particularly hot shooter.

12. In the last minute situations we may change defenses when the opponent has taken time out, hoping to nullify any play or bit of strategy they plan during the time out. We may change for only their first possession of the ball.

These are a few of the reasons we might alter our defense for an opponent or make a change during a game. As the coach matures in the multiple defense game, he will develop the ability to work either to his team's own strength or the opponent's weakness. The coach who has more defensive choices and adjustments to use can enter each game with confidence. He can sell his players on the idea that whatever the opponent gets going for them that night, they will be able to make an adjustment to meet it. A team with pride and confidence in its multiple defense tools is difficult to beat.

PART ONE

MAN-TO-MAN DEFENSES

2

Developing the Individual
for Multiple Defense

It is most important for players to be able to execute individual defensive fundamentals regardless of what defensive system is used. The multiple defense game most certainly breaks down from the start unless each individual can execute the standard defensive moves. Some coaches may prefer to neglect this chapter and the following chapter, regarding them as too elemental. However, most successful coaches are quite careful to teach fundamental details. These details make the multiple defense game work because many things like post defense, overplaying, pressuring the ball, and playing men who do not have the ball are generally consistent throughout all the defenses. When a player masters the many basics, he can learn to adjust into any team defense very quickly.

Our approach to teaching these fundamentals is not necessarily unique. But I want to include a brief study of what we do and of what I feel are important for defenders to master, because being able to perform these moves certainly facilitates adjustability in players. A coach should not try to use multiple defense if he is not willing to drill these basic defensive steps throughout the year. It would be a big mistake to try to move teams in and out of various types and styles of defense who did not have the fundamental habits established. The memory problem would be too much. Moreover, it is doubtful that a team will be strong in any defensive system without these habits. The reason we believe that teams can play several defenses is based on the idea that players can develop an adequate number of *core defensive habits*

27

that are consistent enough in every kind of defense to allow them to play them all. The players do not have to learn several entirely different defenses.

A coach may teach fundamentals of defense differently than we suggest but he can still be successful as long as he teaches them. The coach who neglects teaching the items contained in chapters 2 and 3 in some manner will have little chance for defensive success and especially in using more than one or two defenses. These individual basics make team defense effective.

While we believe a team should be able to play both man-to-man and zone, we think that a successful zone results more often than not because the players are capable of playing good man-to-man defense. Therefore, we begin each season's early practice with man-to-man, whether we feel this will be our basic defense that year or not. Most of our drills will be man-to-man types of drills but they carry over to the zones. As the season progresses we get into our specific zone play, but we hope each player has become a better individual defender by that time due to our stressing man-to-man principles. Depending on the specific year our teams have varied from man-to-man, to zone, or to a press as our number one defense so that we are not advocates of one type over the other.

As a team defense the man-to-man offers a lot of flexibility. The team may press any portion of the court with it. They can pressure all the opponents or only certain ones or only special areas of the floor. On the other hand, instead of pressing they can sag into the middle or collapse on the weak side to help stop the inside game. The man-to-man can be employed at any stage of the game and against any offense. This is even more true when the defensive team is capable of two-timing or trapping. By using overplays and switching, the coach can further complicate the opponent's offensive strategy. The combinations of possible adjustments are innumerable. Therefore, the man-to-man fits quite well into our multiple defense concept, since its adjustability allows many defensive variations.

PSYCHOLOGICAL REQUIREMENTS
FOR THE INDIVIDUAL DEFENDER

In chapter 16 we give mention to the defensive psychology we believe necessary for the team as a whole to have. In addition each individual has a specific task of his own apart from following the team attitude. Regardless of the player's physical talent he will not excel on defense unless he truly wants to be a first-class defender. The prime concern, then, is for each man to develop within himself the desire to play good defense. He has to make it his goal. He must accept playing defense as a challenge to his character and his ability. Character is a primary challenge because any boy who is good enough to play satisfactorily on offense automatically has the ability to play defense on the other end of the floor. We believe that most players can actually be somewhat *better* at defense than they are at offense since it requires fewer natural skills. But it takes quite a bit of mental maturity and determination to play a consistently rugged game of defense. It is the depth of determination in a player that will decide whether he will be able to make the extra effort consistently to keep in front of his man. It takes a tough-minded boy to stay low and to move his feet as well as his opponent. Each man must learn to shape his thinking along the lines of the "Bulldog." That is, he must set himself to the task of taking hold and not letting go until he has completed his job.

Desire, determination and pride in his work are requirements for the strong defender. Unless a boy will feel a twinge of pain when his man beats him, he is still lacking the pride it takes to be at his best. We like to take some of the offensive pressure off of our players by saying from time to time that we believe *anyone* can shoot the ball, but it takes a strong individual to play the kind of defense that gets notice. We sincerely believe that the boys with the most outstanding characters of those we have coached the past several years were very good defensive men. They may have been good scorers also, but they were determined to play on both ends of the court.

Though greatness be reserved for the select few, we advocate that all of our boys should be able to be good defenders. And that is not so much to ask since our players have generally felt that they played against very few even *good* defenders when they reflected on a season. A team with several good defenders has always earned the respect of our boys. And this makes a point for us that we capitalize on: opponents will always respect the good defender and the good defensive unit. Athletes may look with awe at a fine scorer; but they reserve their *respect* for the rebounder and the defender. The fact that any good athlete can be a good defender is a challenge the winning individual cannot resist.

Space does not permit our going into full detail on the fundamentals that are most basic but the following paragraphs will give a significant enough description of what we feel to be important.

Body Position

We prefer the standard boxer stance on defense when guarding a man out on the floor. The only item of possible variance from the general basic stance is that we want our players to assume the *widest* stance that still allows for good mobility. A wide stance makes it more difficult for the opponent to drive around the defender. We do not insist on a particular foot to be forward, though this has not always been the case. We do like a body position that places the weight of the rear end over the feet with a nearly erect trunk position which allows the head to be up rather than down. The position is similar to a person who is lowering himself to sit in a chair. The weight should be evenly distributed on the feet except when guarding a man with the ball. On this occasion we want the weight *forward* toward the front foot. We do this because we have our boys defend so closely on the ballhandler that his only good move is to drive. With the weight on the front foot the defender is ready to push off to retreat hard, cutting off the driver. (See Drill 2 in chapter 5.)

Footwork

We drill the boxer's shuffle steps on defense but in actual play we want our players to get their bodies in front of the offense however they can accomplish it. We no longer do a lot of defensive faking and jabbing. Instead, our defenders try to scoot right up next to the ballhandler as close as possible in order to pressure the ball. We say to get right under the ball; make the ballhandler turn his back. Therefore, the most crucial defensive movement for our individual defenders is the backward *oblique* step to the right or left. That is, since we pressure the ballhandler heavily we must be able to recover hard to either oblique angle. If we have pressured well, we have made it very difficult for the ballhandler to shoot or pass inside. Since his best move would be to drive, we want to be ready for it. Much time must be spent on the backward oblique steps, particularly the first two steps, in order to have effective defenders. (See Drills 1b and 3 in chapter 5.)

Guarding the Ball

In guarding the man with the ball each player must play as tight as he possibly can and still do a reasonable job of containing the drive. If the player has no dribble left, he must be right on him. Even if he has a dribble we want as much pressure as possible. The guarding distance will vary with the relative abilities of the offensive and defensive players, of course, but we want as close a position as we can get. We *expect* our defender on the ball to get beaten by the drive occasionally and we practice our recoveries and traps to make this work to our advantage rather than allow it to beat us. If a defender gets beaten too often and our recoveries do not recover, we will make an adjustment for him.

We usually prefer our men to *overplay* the ballhandler. We practice overplaying to both the inside and outside since there are times one is more advantageous than the other. We overplay by playing the defender's forward foot at least one-half man in the direction of the overplay. In general if no specific overplay is called for, we try to overplay right on a ballhandler's shooting shoulder. That way even if the defender is beaten by the drive he may catch up on the shooting hand side and hamper the shot. At times we overplay a whole team's offense to either the inside or outside. At other times we try to turn the offense to their right or left, or we may overplay a strictly left-handed player toward his strength. Thus, it is best to teach players the ability to overplay to both the right and left. (See Drill 5 in chapter 5.)

Hand and Arm Movement

Moving the hands and arms can help deflect passes, assist the legs in their movement and aid the body in maintaining balance. The hand position varies with the location of the man being defended. In guarding a man *out of scoring range* we like an arms extended, palms up position with the low base. If the offensive player is *in scoring range*, the defender should raise the hand on the same side as his front foot to the offensive player's face area and the other hand to the waist. If the player gives up his dribble, we want our man to move even closer, wave his hands and arms, and use some verbal defense as well. (See Drill 4 in chapter 5.)

The arms and hands should be thrust vigorously in the direction of movement to give more quickness, but the best use of the upper limbs involves discouraging shots and deflecting passes.

We want at least a finger tip to touch each pass, if possible; it leads to many interceptions. Concentrating on the ball helps a great deal to accomplish this. Proper arm position is more of a factor, however in deflecting passes. We have just discussed the desired use of the hands when guarding the ballhandler. Successfully guarding a man without the ball necessitates knowing two arm positions. One, if the defender is *pressuring* his man out on the floor he will usually do so by closing his stance in the direction of his man and extending the arm nearest the ball almost into the passing lane between his man and the ball. The defender's hand will be turned with the thumb down, opening the palm to the ball. Pressuring in closer to the goal would force the defender to be right in the pass lane. Two, if the defender is sagging off his man he will open his stance toward the ball. The arm nearest the ball will be extended back toward the basket area with the thumb up, again keeping the palm open to the ball. The other arm will also be extended in each case toward the defender's man.

Some coaches have their boys use only the open stance or only the closed stance. This is all right, but regardless, the arm and hand position is very important to bothering the passing game of the opponent. (See Drill 6 in chapter 5.)

DEFENDING PLAYERS ONE PASS FROM THE BALL

Ball in the Backcourt

Defenders play one step off of the passing lane from the ball to their man and must play closer to the ball. That is, if the offensive man is only ten feet from the ball, the defender should be about seven feet from it. If he is as far as thirty or forty feet, the defender can play as much as ten or fifteen feet closer to the ball, but still only one step from the direct passing lane. (Diagrams 2-1 and 2-2).

Guard Play at Half-Court

Guards vary in their defensive position when not guarding the ball. If the team is *pressing*, the guard defending his man who is only one pass from the ball will have his hand nearest the ball extended and will be only one step off of the pass lane and about

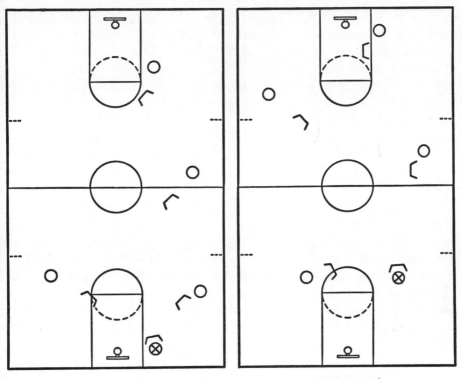

Diagram 2-1   Diagram 2-2

one or two steps closer to the ball than his man is. (These positions are relative to the abilities of players and represent the ideal position.) The player must not be right *in* the lane because he wants the lane to *appear* to be open to set up his steal. If the team is *not pressing* the guard would open up his body toward the ball. He would have one arm point in toward the post area and the farthest arm from the ball would point at his man. As mentioned, some coaches have their guards use this open body position even when pressing, and we find no real fault with this. (Diagrams 2-3 and 2-4.)

Forward Play at Half-Court

In guarding men on the wing and corner areas our players play a tight, almost fronting, position. If the man moves into the post area the defender applies the post defense rules, of course. Thus, a defender would be in a fronting position in the area from

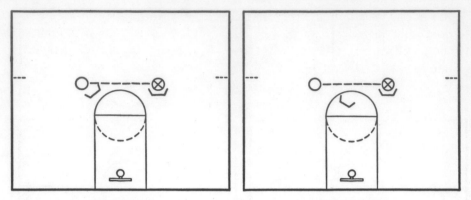

Diagram 2-3   Diagram 2-4

the goal to ten or twelve feet away, but from that point to about twenty to twenty-two feet from the goal the defender plays only his hand ahead of his man. The hand nearest the ball should be right in the passing lane, and the body a step closer to ball than the offense is. His back arm will extend out to act as a feeler to let him know if the offensive player reverses. (Diagram 2-5.) If the man backdoors toward the goal, our man will turn right with him (facing him) to prevent him from getting a return pass. Once the offensive man has moved out of normal scoring range (past twenty feet or so) our defender will drop off of the pass lane unless we are trying to shut off that man entirely from the ball. The basic idea is that we do not want a forward to have the ball within twenty feet of the goal.

When the offensive forward does receive the ball we want our men to get right on him in an effort to prevent his doing anything positive with the ball. We try to prevent any open shot or inside pass. At best we force the man to turn his back and pass outside. If he drives we are over-playing to make him go the way we desire and we hope to pick him up with our team defense. (See Drill 6 in chapter 5 for guard, post, and forward position drills.)

Post Play

In defending a man in the post area we like to play in front of all post men who are within ten or twelve feet of the goal. We try to get on the baseline side if we get caught behind a man in deep and we play him on the baseline side until we can get back in front again. (Diagram 2-6.) In other words we try to keep the ball out of the post area as much as possible. There are other ways to play the post that a coach can successfully employ in certain situations such as fronting even to the fifteen-foot range or, on the other hand, nearly always playing beside the post man so as never to forfeit rebounding position. (Diagram 2-7.)

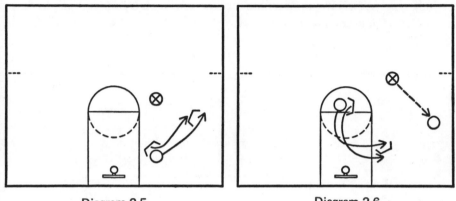

Diagram 2-5   Diagram 2-6

Regardless of what position a player begins playing, he will find himself guarding a man near the goal occasionally. It is important that each man know that he must gradually straighten up as he gets closer to the goal on defense. He must straighten and try to avoid yielding ground as his opponent gets close to the goal, with or without the ball. A man crouched low and who yields ground will be of little defensive help under the basket.

GUARDING A MAN TWO PASSES FROM THE BALL

The toughest defensive teams we have seen were those who were good at defending men two passes from the ball. They were able to help the aggressive defenders who were pressuring the ball and were in a position to beat any cutter into the goal area. To stay in the defensive game even when his man is not involved is a sign of a top-notch defender.

Guard Play

When defending a man in the guard area the defender must

turn toward the ball and sag into the free throw lane to help plug up the middle. He should maintain visual contact with both the ball and his man if possible. If a choice becomes necessary, he will watch his man and then pick up sight of the ball when he can. Seeing both the man and the ball can be accomplished by dropping back and turning so as to be able to look approximately half-way between the man and ball to see both by using peripheral vision. (Diagram 2-8.) Some coaches call this "splitting to see the ball."

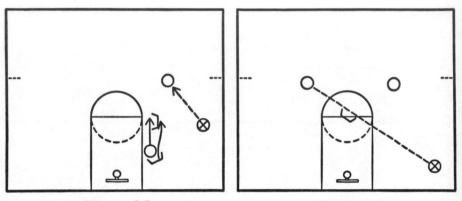

Diagram 2-7   Diagram 2-8

Forward Play

While defending a man two passes away in the forward area, the defender has to turn toward the ball and move toward the free throw lane. We try to sag as far in toward the goal as possible. By standing with the body only one step off the pass lane he can still get in front of his man if he cuts to the ball. The defender must open toward the ball with his hand nearest the ball pointing at the ball while the other hand points toward his man. Again visual contact may be maintained by looking at a mid-point but if it must be broken with either the man or the ball momentarily, the man should be watched. The defender should be alert to steal or deflect any lob passes to the post man. He must be ready to get in front of any driver to 'tne goal, especially the other forward's man who may drive the baseline occasionally. As mentioned he has to defend any cut his own man may make to the ball or goal. (Diagrams 2-9 through 2-12.)

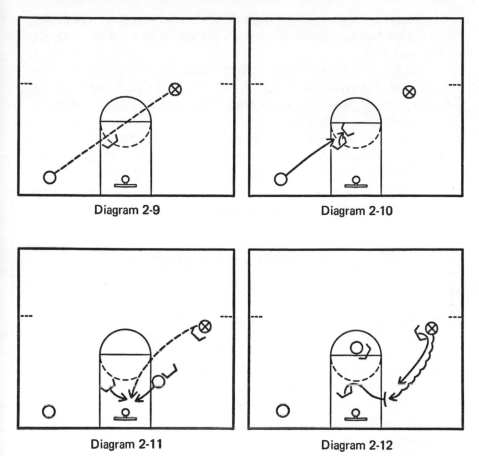

Diagram 2-9

Diagram 2-10

Diagram 2-11

Diagram 2-12

GENERAL RULES FOR DEFENDERS

This diagram will help clarify the previous rules. These simple guidelines are very useful. (Diagram 2-13.)

Player 1—guard position one pass away rule. He will move toward the ball and see the ball and his man. If he is *pressing,* he would be only one step off the pass lane from the ball. If he is playing *regular,* he would drop a little further in order to help stop. the middle. He should stunt up and back, but he must stop the *inside* drive by 2's man, especially when 2 is overplaying *outside.*

Player 2—the man guarding the ball rule. He must play the ball tight, try to deflect any pass, and try to prevent a good pass inside. He must push the ball either inside or outside, whichever one he is told to do.

Player 3—high post position rule. He tries to get in front or at least get a hand in front of his man. He wants to keep the ball out of the post area.

Player 4—forward position two passes from the ball rule. He must move into the lane and look for lobs to the post. He must get in front of his man's cut to the ball. He must be ready to stop 5's man on the drive to the goal.

Player 5—forward position one pass from the ball rule. He must play even with his man while he is in the scoring area and stand a step closer to the ball. He must prevent his man from getting a pass in the scoring area. He must stop the *outside* drive of 2's man when we tell the guard to overplay the *inside*.

BALL IN FORWARD POSITION

With the ball at the forward spot, the rules would correlate with the aforementioned guidelines. (Diagram 2-14.)

Players 1 and 4—two passes away rule. They look at the ball and their man and sag into the middle. They are ready to stop any cut to the ball and to help in the post area. Player 4 is ready to help on 5's man's drive to the goal if necessary.

Player 2—one pass away rule. He drops back just as the ball is thrown and falls to approximately ball level. He will stop 5's man's drive to the inside. If he is pressing, he would stay one step from the pass lane from 5's man to his.

Player 3—low post rule. He tries to get in front by playing on the baseline side.

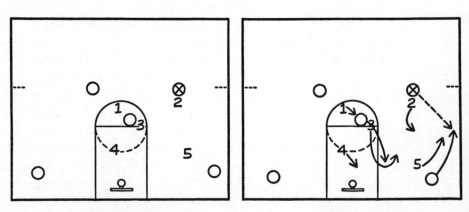

Diagram 2-13   Diagram 2-14

Player 5—guarding the ball rule. He gets right under the ballhandler and forces him inside or outside, whichever way we are to play this time. He prevents any inside passes and tries to deflect any pass.

Another guideline we have used to simplify the teaching of our defense to our boys has been to draw three semi-circular areas on the floor to label them as scoring zones. (Diagram 2-15.) It has proved to be very effective.

In the *twelve-foot area* each player must try to front his man so as to prevent him from getting the ball in the area. Do not allow your man to have the ball in this area. Give every effort to get in front.

In the *twenty-one-foot area* pressure the ballhandler hard. Forwards one pass away have at least one hand between their man and the ball. Do not allow him to get the ball if possible. Battle with him for the spot at which he wants to get the ball. Force him out further. If your man is two passes away, drop toward the twelve-foot area. Guards who are pressing and their man is one pass away should be one step from the pass lane and a step or two closer to the ball. If the defense is not pressing, the guard would drop closer toward the *twelve-foot area.* Guards two passes away, drop toward the *twelve-foot area.*

In the safe area beyond twenty-one feet pressure the ball. Push it either inside or outside as directed. If there are no specific overplay directions, play the shooting shoulder hard.

DEFENDING THE BASIC INDIVIDUAL MOVES

Defending the Driver

In guarding a driver in the front court we usually are trying to turn the offense a particular direction. Basically, however, it is good policy to force a dribbler away from the basket. We hope to prevent any driver from taking a straight path to the goal. We *never* want our player to run alongside a dribbler, pacing himself with him. Once a defender is out of position we want him to run as fast as possible to regain a good defensive frontal position on his man. To do this he must pick out a spot ahead of the dribbler where he can cut him off and run to it rather than run alongside the dribbler. If someone else picks up his man before he recovers, he will either take that man's opponent or trap, whatever the situation calls for. We will mention more on this under *Recoveries*. (See Drill 7 in chapter 5.)

Defending the Passer

We try to get both hands up against the feeder, especially if he has no dribble. Even if a player can still dribble but he is in a particular offense where he is strictly a feeder, we will crowd right up to him with both arms up to make him do something else. Our goal is to *deflect* each pass. (See Drill 4 in chapter 5.)

Defending the Man Who Just Passed

This man can be very dangerous in most offenses. As soon as a pass is made the man guarding the passer backs up right away and opens up toward the direction of the pass. He anticipates any cut or screen. If the ball were passed over or behind him, we like for the defender to drop back until he is nearly at ball level or at least until he can see the ball and his man well. (Diagram 2-16.) This will allow him to help plug up the middle and also will help him from being easy prey to cuts and screens. (See Drills 6b, c and d in chapter 5.)

Defending the Cutter

As stated we try to keep the defender's body between the man and the goal and only one step off his direct path to the ball.

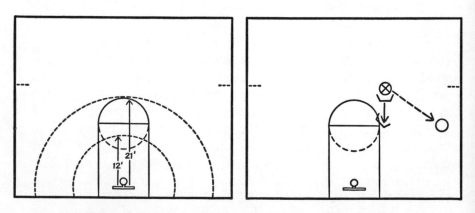

Diagram 2-15   Diagram 2-16

(Diagram 2-17.) We want our defender to be in a position so that he can be in front of any good cut to the ball or goal. In cases where the offensive player is two passes from the ball, the defender would be several steps closer to the ball than his man is. We hope to delay the timing of every cutter by being in front. We accomplish this by sliding one or two steps as the cutter breaks; then the defender turns his rear into the cutter's waist to check him off, and then will try to stay in front. (Diagram 2-18.) (See Drill 8 in chapter 5.)

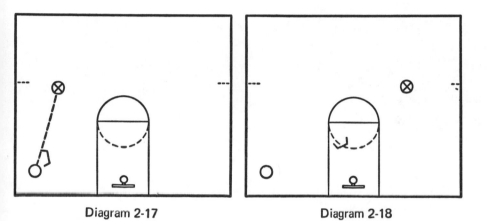

Diagram 2-17   Diagram 2-18

Defending Against the Screen

We want the man who is guarding the screener to inform the man likely to be screened of the possible screen as early as possible. Each man should always be anticipating screens by looking and by having the hand nearest the direction of his movement out as a feeler hand in case his teammates fail to warn him. In general, we switch on all screens in the scoring area and will have rules which may vary with different teams to cover other screens and crosses. With a team that has balanced height we will do a lot of switching. Where there are height variations of significance we will rule our defense to cut down the number of switches. The rules must fit the team and the drills must fit the rules. We most often try to avoid getting screened by playing over the top of the screen. The best way to accomplish this is to try to arch the back and throw the leading leg and the hips forward toward the ballhandler as he nears the screener. This will prevent the hips from getting hit by the screener and will allow the defender to slide right over the screen unless it is set perfectly. Assuredly if the defender does get screened in the scoring area, we want the switch made. The defender on the screener must anticipate the switch by being tight on his man and leaning in the direction of the cut so as to be able to jump-switch in front quickly. (Drill 9 in chapter 5.)

3

Defending with the
Basic Two- and Three-Man Moves

While it is necessary for players to be able to defend with the various one-man maneuvers to make the multiple defense system more easily taught, it is equally important that they be able to employ the several two- and three-man moves that occur in nearly every game. When the team is able to execute all of the fundamental one-, two-, and three-man moves, they are capable of making five-man team adjustments. But, the coach that attempts adjusting his defenses back and forth with a team that has not been drilling daily for many weeks on the basic moves will have a very confused and ill-prepared team. Perhaps our approach to defending these offensive exercises is not new to the experienced coach. Regardless, the point of including the material is to emphasize just how important the drilling of these throughout the season is to the multiple defense game. For that matter, we feel they must be worked at just the same even if the coach contemplates having only one good type of defense.

THE BASIC MOVES

Give and Go

One principle we stress which is common to all defenses is for the defender to drop quickly to nearly the level of the ball if it is passed behind him. By following this principle the defender can go far toward preventing the successful give and go. (Diagram 3-1.)

The defender must drop immediately, turn slightly in the direction of the pass and try to locate the ball. But he must *not* turn completely and take his eyes entirely off his man. The "head-turner" is a dead man against the give and go. The defender should try to get his body in front of his man's cut to the goal, if possible. He must be sure to get at least a hand between his man and the ball. The man guarding the new ballhandler helps by putting pressure on the ball. (See Drill 8c in chapter 5.)

Screen and Roll

We want the man screened to roll with his body facing the screener and turn his head in the direction of the ball. (Diagram 3-2.) He would make contact when the feeler hand touches the screener, turn with him toward the goal and stick his other hand, the one nearest the ball, in between his man and the passer. In this position he would be facing the direction of the goal, the same as the cutter. He must keep his body between the ball and the rolling man. The man who switches to the ballhandler must jump out into his path on the "hard" switch if he can. To accomplish the hard switch, the switcher edges out a half-step in the direction he will have to switch as he sees the cutter approach. He must be tight on his man and keep his hand nearest his own man right on that man's hip as he anticipates the possible switch situation. If he does switch he pushes off from his man and throws his leg out wide in the path of the man he wants to switch to. He tries to get his body right in his new man's path. He will then pressure the man so as to prevent a successful pass to the roller. To do this hard switch successfully, the key is proper anticipation of the screen. The only

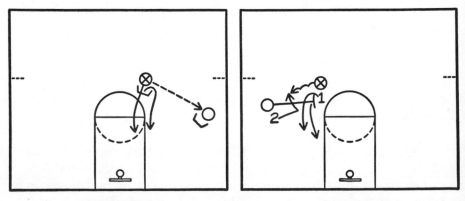

Diagram 3-1   Diagram 3-2

pitfall is when a man defending the ball switches prematurely to a cutter and his man fakes the hand-off and is then wide open. The defense will not fall prey to a fake hand-off if they remember the rule of switching *to* the ball, never *from* the ball. He must be sure his man hands off on the hand-off screen and roll play before the switches. If the defender is screened while guarding the ball, he must switch but this involves a new man switching *to* the ball so the rule still applies, though it may seem not to. It is the only case in which a defender leaves the ball, but it is easy to remember because the man guarding the ball is screened and has no choice. The point is, *stay on the ballhandler* in screen situations until the man gives up the ball or until you are screened off of it.

Guards Splitting the Post

We like for *both* men involved in the split to *drop to the level of the ball* and then switch men with each other as the men split (Diagram 3-3.) That way the man guarding the post need not switch. The only real problem occurs on a fake-split when the second cutter goes right behind the first one (Diagram 3-4.) The

Diagram 3-3   Diagram 3-4

defense must be alert to this possibility. The cutter's man may be able to recover and catch up or the post man's defender will have to switch if the man is given the ball. (See Drill 9f in chapter 5.)

Forward-Guard Splitting the Post

We defend this move differently than the guard-guard split to avoid the defensive mismatch. Furthermore, it is difficult to defend the same way. Therefore we play against the team that uses this move by overplaying inside on the potential forward cutter as 2 does in Diagram 3-5 and by overplaying the guard's outside as 1 does. This prevents the splitting move or else pushes the cutters out, leaving room to go over the post man. (See Drill 9f in chapter 5.)

The Clear

If an offensive player clears out of the area between the ballhandler and the goal, the man guarding him must yell out to inform his teammate defending the ballhandler. (Diagram 3-6.) The defender on the ball should quickly loosen up and overplay the outside. The defender who was cleared out should see if he can stay near the goal to help out. The other defenders must also be alert to assist. Many times the offensive player who clears goes out of the play entirely and is no threat. In these cases there is no need for the defender to follow him. The coach can observe what counter-move the opponent does with the man who clears. If none is used, the clear may be stopped easier. (See Drill 9g in chapter 5.)

The Shuffle Cut

There is no excuse for being surprised by the screen away from the ball. The skilled defender should be in a position to anticipate the screen, particularly after the first time the move is used against him (Diagram 3-7). Against the shuffle our defender,

Diagram 3-5   Diagram 3-6

2, is in a position guarding a man two passes from the ball. The defender should be able to jump over the screen and stay between the cutter and the pass in most cases if he starts soon enough. We want him to beat the cutter into the free throw lane. The post defender can help by stepping out from beside the post screener to "show" himself in a fake switch. The cutter will usually flare out wider when the post shows and this will allow our defender on him more room to avoid the screen. If the post man has to switch to prevent a lay-in, he will. We also want our defender on the ballhandler to help by putting pressure on the ball extremely hard because he is most dangerous as a feeder in the shuffle. (See Drill 9c in chapter 5.)

The Stack

At times we do nothing special to defend stacked players. But if a team is hurting us by executing the move well, we go into a special adjustment. In Diagram 3-8 players 4 and 5 are stacked.

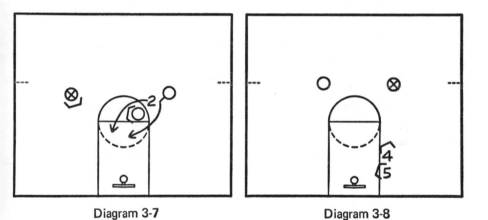

Diagram 3-7   Diagram 3-8

The man guarding 4 will take the man that breaks to the wing to get open and the player guarding 5 will stop any counter-move to the goal. Normally our taller, or stronger man will defend player 5 in this situation. Note that the man guarding 4 must front him.

The Button Hook

This move is a relatively difficult one to defend. (Diagram 3-9.) The cutter, player 2, moves to the goal as 1 dribbles toward him. The man defending 2 must try to stay between his man and the ball. Otherwise, 2 will button hook abruptly near the goal and the defender will be behind. The player guarding the ballhandler must keep pressure on the ball in order to help prevent the good pass.

Diagram 3-9

SWITCHING

Rules regarding switching while playing the man-to-man will vary in each team from year to year. A very strong team may get by with few switches, but most teams, regardless of ability, will find it necessary to switch often due to the skill with which offenses are run. We have followed certain general rules for years but have used some variations each year. Basically, we switch on every successful screen in the scoring area. We will instruct our players to try to avoid the screen, but we always switch if the opponent puts on a successful screen in the twenty-foot range. Also, we generally allow our guards to switch with one another on any screens or crossing movements their men may make, whether the ball is in either of their possession or not.

We try to keep our forwards from switching with our guards but do not try to keep them from switching with each other or our center. All successful screens in the scoring area necessitate a switch whether the ball is involved or not. We instruct our player defending a screening opponent to anticipate that the screener will pick off his teammate and so be *ready* to switch. But we tell the defender being screened to try to *avoid* being blocked off so that the screen is not successful, making a switch unnecessary. Talking on defense and playing good off-the-ballhandler defense will help negate many screening attempts. (See Drill 9 in chapter 5.)

There is no one magic way to play man-to-man. Certain methods—sag or press, switch or not—will work better with certain personnel than with others. The coach must be aware of the merits of each style. We try to adjust as we see fit. The following is another guideline we have used regarding switching:

Guard-to-guard screens. Switch on all crosses or screens unless instructed otherwise for a particular game. Switch out hard and stop the play. Draw the offensive foul.

Guard-to-forward screens. Try to avoid switching either by playing over the top of the screen in close to the goal (twenty feet and in) and by sliding through out further on the floor. If screened off, switch and roll with the screener keeping a hand between him and the ball. The forward must hard switch.

Forward-to-center or forward screens. Switch if successfully screened. Always keep in front. Try to develop the ability to anticipate the switch before it comes. A good defender is one who learns to anticipate his opponent's next move, whether it be a cut, screen, pass, or shot. Then he makes the effort to stop that move by being ahead of the play and forcing another move.

Fake Switching

The back men, centers especially, can help avoid switching by using the fake switch called "showing" earlier. That is, when they see a cutter approach in an attempt to rub off a man, the faker acts like he is going to hard switch. This causes the offensive cutter to flare out enough for our defender to get through over the top and avoid the switch. This is a good move to help against the shuffle cut as mentioned. Just by stepping out into the cutter's path enough to show himself, the fake switcher can help his teammate considerably. And if he is actually forced to switch, he is already half-way there. This move is successful in preventing a driver from going on further toward the goal in most instances, also.

Tips for Switching on Defense

To further simplify our teaching on switching, we have

compiled the following list of suggestions that we give to each of our players.

1. If you are screened, take the screener yourself.
2. Automatically switch on guard crosses or guard-to-guard screens unless you are instructed otherwise for a special reason.
3. If there is no tall opposing center, the forwards inside can switch without worry. If a 6'7" or taller center is involved, we may have one man to stay with him all the time, unless he is screened perfectly.
4. When you switch and your new man rolls, you have to roll your body with his and extend your arm in between this man and the ball to deflect a return pass as you follow him in.
5. Play the men near the ball tight; if you are too far behind your man and he screens, you won't be able to switch in time to stop a jump shot behind his screen.
6. Switch hard; that is, bounce out from behind the screener right into the dribbler's or cutter's path. Make him stop or charge you or go another way. After taking him drop back just a little if he still has his dribble.
7. Once you begin a switch and the offensive men cross, *you must go through with it.* Do not confuse your teammate.
8. Switch back to your original man only when you are sure the ball will not be involved with either man.
9. Learn to *anticipate* screens and try to avoid them. Overplaying and using the feeler hand helps.
10. Do not switch from your man if he has the ball unless you are screened. Switch *to* the ball, not *from* the ball. Be sure your man passes the ball or you are screened before you leave him.

TRAPPING

It is appropriate to bring in the basics of trapping here because it is necessary for any team which hopes to have multiple defenses to be able to trap out of any of their defenses. The methods of trapping are the same whether done from a man-to-man or zone. Although the trap is executed by two men, the entire defensive team must react if trapping is to be effective.

Trapping involves going from a basic one-on-one defense to a situation in which two men attack the ballhandler and the rest of the area is momentarily zoned. Regardless of the style of defense played there are four basic trap situations: the guard-to-guard, the guard-to-forward, the forward-to-guard, and the forward-deep post. Coaches will vary in their use of these traps with respect to particular spots on the floor where a trap might be used, the special keys to call the trap and the timing used. But the actual traps are the same. Some coaches will teach only one or two instead of all four basic traps. There are many ways to use the traps; when a team knows how to trap, there are a lot of pressure tactics they can use with every defense. (See Drill 12 in chapter 5.)

How to Trap

We insist that the man who goes to two-time be able to get to the ballhandler with about *three quick steps* or less. We feel that if the trapper has to travel very far the offense will have time to adjust to the trap and beat it. If the elements of quickness and surprise are lost, the defense will get beaten. We like for the trapper to spread out in a wide base as he makes his last step to trap. He places his foot nearest his own defensive teammate close to that teammate to prevent the ballhandler from splitting between them. We want to prevent that split. The trappers avoid getting right up against the ballhandler. They keep two or three feet from the man in the trap while they yell and wave both arms. It is important to keep the arms and hands *up*, not *out* toward the ballhandler. This helps prevent reaching in, slapping, and fouling. *We never want to foul in a trap.* What we hope for is either a five-second call, a stolen pass or a deflected pass. We do not look for the outright steal or tie-up. Keeping a little distance between the trappers and the ballhandler helps prevent fouls, makes splitting more difficult and gives a better shot at deflecting a pass. The man still feels pressure in this predicament.

Keys for Trapping

We try not to over-use the traps. We like for the ballhandler to be in certain situations before we spring a trap except in our desperation defense. To begin with we instruct as to whether we are to use the trap or not for this particular game or specific period in the game. We seldom just turn them loose. If we are using the trap we trap at half-court when any of the following conditions are met: (a) A ballhandler is driven into a second defender; or (b) the ballhandler turns his back to the man who can go to two-time him; or (c) a screen and roll situation occurs; or (d) the ballhandler is off-balance, as in a corner, or (e) he gets into a deep-post spot along the baseline. All of these situations will be illustrated in the following paragraphs as the specific trapping methods are described. A team may use one or two or all of these keys.

Prime Spots in the Front Court for Trapping

Although a successful trap may be sprung at various places on the floor the four corners provide the best areas. Other prime spots are on top of the key on the guard-guard cross, and at the forward angles on the screen and roll, or when a dribbler heads for the base line and turns his back on potential trappers. An automatic trap spot for us has been the deep-post trap near the base line (Diagram 3-10).

Guard-to-Guard Traps

In the guard-guard traps the forwards must *float* to try to steal the next pass and the post man must zone the goal area.

In Diagram 3-11 the offensive guard dribbled into player 2 and 2 trapped with 1. Note how 4 and 5 float to steal the pass and

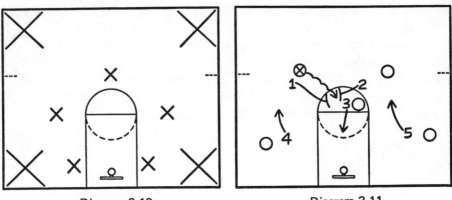

Diagram 3-10   Diagram 3-11

3 zones the crucial goal area. In Diagram 3-12 the ballhandler turned his back on player 2 who trapped. In Diagram 3-13, 1 and 2 trapped on a guard-guard cross. In all cases 4 and 5 float and 3 zones the goal.

Guard-to-Forward Trap

In all guard-forward traps the other guard floats to steal, the

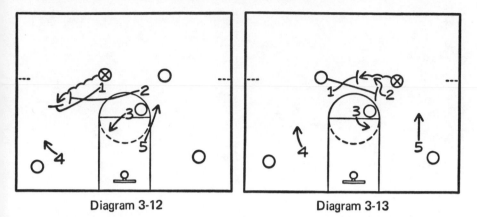

Diagram 3-12   Diagram 3-13

post is alert to steal and the *farthest man* from the trap (the other forward) zones the goal. Diagram 3-14 shows 2 trapping with 5 as the dribbler turns his back to 2. In Diagram 3-15, 2 jumps 5's man in the corner because 5 forced him into an off-balance situation. In each case all players react the same way.

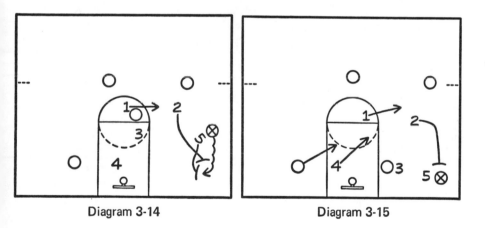

Diagram 3-14   Diagram 3-15

Forward-to-Guard Trap

In Diagram 3-16 players 2 and 5 have trapped a screen and roll move. Player 4 zones the goal while the post defender, 3, and the other guard float to steal. In Diagram 3-17 player 2 has gotten his man to give up his dribble and turn his back so 5 traps with him. This could occur when the ballhandler drives hard into player 5, too. Players 1 and 3 float to steal and 4 zones the goal as in Diagram 3-16.

Diagram 3-16   Diagram 3-17

Forward-Deep-Post Trap

In the trap the forward was beaten by the drive. But the opposite forward converges to trap in the deep-post area. The guards 1 and 2 play for the possible release passes, while the post man stops up the goal area. (Diagram 3-18.)

Occasionally the post man will have to form the trap with the forward. If this occurs, The weak side forward will try to take the post man's place. The guards will move the same as before. (See Drill 12 in chapter 5.)

Trap Lanes

It is good for the team to realize that regardless of which players form the trap, the slides to cover the possible escape pass are alike in both man-to-man and zone. Diagram 3-19 shows the court divided into three verticle trap lanes. All traps will occur in an outside lane or the middle lane. If an outside lane trap is set, the nearest players will cover the two floating areas, the down pass and the flat or back pass. The fifth man will protect the goal. (Diagram 3-20.) If the trap is sprung in the middle lane the floating areas will be the two outside lanes adjacent to the ball. The goal will be protected as always by the remaining man. (Diagram 3-21.) Thus, a *triangle of two floaters and a goalie* is set with each trap. By going over the traps in Diagrams 3-11 through 3-18 the observer can see that trap slides can be taught rather easily. Players must react to fill the float areas just as the trap is set. As long as the goal is protected, the defense can afford the risk involved.

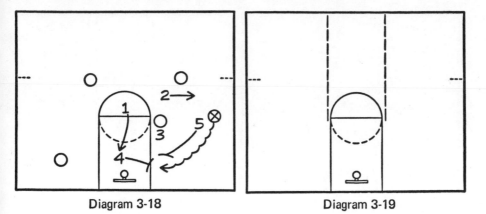

Diagram 3-18   Diagram 3-19

The Fake Trap

After a few traps have been sprung it is wise to bluff a trap and get back to one's own man to try to pick off any quick pass the offense might be tricked into throwing. Traps should not be used too much. It is important that the offense make one of the key mistakes and for the defense to be able to spring the trap quickly. Otherwise, a good team will make a trapping team suffer. It is an easy thing for the coach to see if the traps are not working. Therefore, it is good for the traps to be used as an extra part to the regular defense so that they can be added or subtracted without changing the basic defense, depending on the need and effectiveness against any given team..

RECOVERING

If a steal does not result, the defense must recover. Whoever ends up protecting the goal prevents a lay-in by zoning the goal while the rest of the players *scramble* to get their men back. For an instant during the trap the men give up their man-to-man assignments and zone the ball, but in recovering get back to their men. Some teams have used the trap to key going into a zone for the rest of that particular time down the floor, but most go back to the man-to-man in recovering.

To summarize trapping, the most important thing to realize when teaching pressing and trapping is that the defenders will not always be in such neat positions as described here on paper. For that reason players should understand the whole idea, not just a

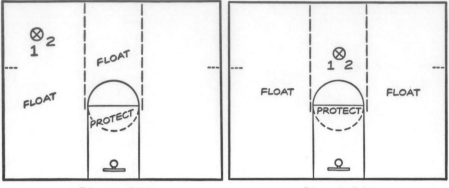

Diagram 3-20   Diagram 3-21

specific move or two. Pressing and trapping will be detailed again in Part Three with considerably more elaboration. For now, let me say that by reviewing the traps shown in this chapter a coach may observe that they have this in common: two men trap, and a triangle is formed whereby the goal area is protected and the two possible passes on either side of the trap are played for by the nearest men who can get there. When a team realizes the overall simplicity involved, they learn it easier.

As may be imagined it is important to drill these traps and for all players to be alert to anticipate traps because if only one man fails to make his move, the opponent will have an easy opening. If each player can keep an eye on his man and the ball, they will not be caught flat very often.

The wise coach will not neglect to drill his players on the basic one-, two-, and three-man defensive moves in the early season practices and to brush up periodically on them throughout the year. Players who can execute the defensive moves discussed in these last two chapters can play every defense in basketball.

4

Making the Man-to-Man Multiple
at Half-Court

After the coach has acquainted his players for a few practices regarding the basic one-, two-, and three-man moves, the next step in the multiple defense system is to develop a good man-to-man defense. Although our use of zones and presses mixed with the man-to-man has really made our multiple defenses work, it has been noted before that it is possible to adjust any one of the three types in various ways to lend a multiple effect. This chapter will illustrate how to adjust with the man-to-man.

Before the man-to-man can be altered to suit changing situations, the coach must decide what style of man-to-man defense he will have his team play. There are three separate styles the coach may select: the straight man-to-man, the automatic switching, or the ruled switching. He may ultimately adjust his defense in several different ways, but once he has decided which of the three basic styles he will teach that year, he will normally want to stay with it all year. Although many defensive changes may be made during each game and throughout the season, the coach will find it troublesome to try to get his players to change their basic style. That is, they will not be able to switch on screens for one game and not the next. Adjust anywhere else, but *not* with your switch rules.

THE THREE STYLES OF MAN-TO-MAN

The *straight* man-to-man is just what the name implies.

Ideally, there will be no switching in this style. But in actual practice players must switch to stop the scoring play near the goal. To play the straight man-to-man effectively a team must have strong individual defenders. Due to the complexity of today's offensive game not many teams employ this defense as they once used to do. We have found use for this defense for a few minutes at a time in early season practice just to make our boys more aware of their individual defensive responsibilities. It also helps identify the ones who want to play defense.

On the other end of the defensive pole is the *automatic switch*. Some coaches have their players switch on every screen whether the ball be involved or not, while others limit the switch to when the ball is in the play. Teams with balanced height can switch without fear of mismatches; size variations cause mismatches. While it makes it difficult for the coach to nail down individual responsibilities when many switches are allowed, it becomes a tough defense to crack when executed well. It can be alternated with a zone effectively to cause the offense a great deal of confusion.

The *ruled switching* man-to-man is a compromise between the two previously mentioned styles. By setting rules to cover the several screening and crossing situations the coach can get the best of the first two styles put into one defense. This is the way most coaches use the man-to-man, but some coaches fail to make the switch rules clear to their players and this can ruin the team defense.

The players can master simple switch rules quickly through drilling and develop an effective defense. We have chosen this as our basic man-to-man style each year, whether man-to-man was our number one defense or not. We have not changed our rules during the year once we became set; however, from year to year we have used different switch rules. Depending on personnel, the coach must decide where his team can or must switch. Some of the choices of rules are as follows:

1. Guards may switch with each other on screens (and possibly crosses), but not with the inside men.
2. Switching may be allowed within a certain radius from the goal, but not beyond that distance selected.
3. Forwards and centers may switch automatically with each other or only in a have-to situation.
4. Guards may switch with forwards in a given situation or area. Post men may be excluded or included in this.

The coach may select one or two of the above rules or he may choose to use some of his own. We mentioned in our discussion of switching in chapter 3 two of the combinations we have frequently used. Regardless of the rule or rules selected, the coach must teach them well through both verbal and drill repetitions.

After the coach decides on the basic man-to-man style and his players begin to become skilled in executing it, he can teach ways in which they can adjust the defense for the multiple effect. There are four team positions and several more specifically individual adjustments that we have used considerably to help give our man-to-man more versatility. It is easy to spend a little practice time periodically directed toward using some of these adjustments after the players are reasonably accustomed to their switch rules.

OUR FOUR TEAM POSITIONS

We describe the four team positions we have in mind as follows: regular, pressing or laning, sagging or containing, and trapping. One of these would be the way we start a game, so there would be a choice of any of the remaining three to which we could adjust. Keep in mind that these adjustments do not affect the man-to-man style regarding switching because that remains constant throughout.

The "regular" positioning is labeled as such because players are in between pressing and sagging at that point and we can communicate the positions we want in just one word with this terminology. Diagrams 4-1 through 4-3 illustrate the regular

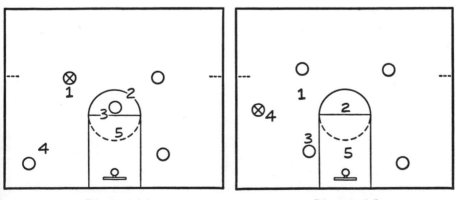

Diagram 4-1   Diagram 4-2

positions with the ball in three different spots on the floor. In each case the defender on the ballhandler is pressuring the ball. Observe that each guard is two or three steps back from his man when his man does not have the ball. The post man plays a different body position in each diagram. In Diagram 4-1 the post man is very high and so the defender is beside him. In Diagram 4-2 our post defender is fronting and in Diagram 4-3 he tries to regain position on the base line side. The men one and two passes from the ball are applying the rules to cover those situations as discussed in chapter 2. It is simply as labeled, regular positioning. It will become more clear as we discuss the other positions.

The Pressing Positions

The defense will pick up the ballhandlers at the half line or even a bit in the back court. As opposed to the regular or normal man-to-man, the laning defense places men more in a position of being *between the ball and the man* than directly between the goal and the man. Some coaches will have the guards play regular and the forwards to lane or vice versa but the five-man pressing defense is played as pictured below. (Diagram 4-4 through 4-6.) The defenders do *not play completely* between the man and the ball but they are more mindful of the pass lane than of basket position. They still try to keep from getting beaten to the goal and must try to regain rebounding position when a shot is taken. Their purpose is to break up the offensive pattern, complicate the passing game and push the offense out on the floor by playing the pass lanes. Compare the positions with the regular defense. Note

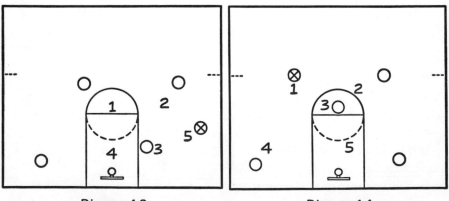

Diagram 4-3   Diagram 4-4

the big change that all players *one pass* from the ball are *nearer the pass lane* and their man in the lane pressure defense than in the regular positions. The post man is more aggressive to front, but there is not much difference in positioning when guarding a man *two passes* from the ball. In each case the ball is pressured.

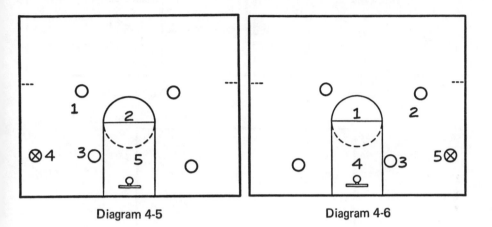

Diagram 4-5   Diagram 4-6

The Sagging Positions

The main variation in the sagging man-to-man is that all men are quicker to drop inside to plug up the middle. Players guarding the ball one and two passes away will try to hamper the inside play by sagging farther from their man when he does not have the ball. Against a team with a good inside attack this defense can be quite effective. Also, late in the game when the defense is ahead on the scoreboard, this can force the opponent to shoot long to catch up. Pressure can still be put on the ballhandler as in the other defensive positions. (Diagrams 4-7 through 4-9.)

Trapping Positions

The four traps that a team may employ at half-court have already been described in chapter 3. When we want to adjust our team to the trapping game we can signal it from the bench or from a time-out. With experience by late season the players may key traps themselves. Each coach must decide whether he will allow his team to use all four traps or only some of them.

It is an asset to have the defense able to play the four different team positions. The team can move in and out from

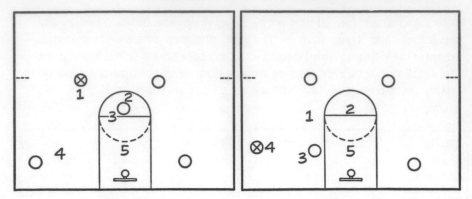

Diagram 4-7   Diagram 4-8

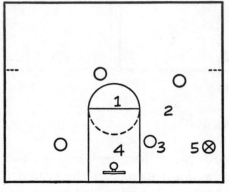

Diagram 4-9

pressing to sagging, from sagging to trapping, or any combination. It is possible to play either of the first three team positions and use the traps when the situation allows. Thus, with little extra burden, the team can learn to play its man-to-man with enough variation to alter the offensive tempo. The fundamentals will vary only slightly so the players do not have a lot of extra material to remember. But the changes of positioning will cause the offense to adjust its game each time. In nearly every case the offense has to adjust more than the defense. This is a plus for the defense.

OTHER DEFENSIVE ADJUSTMENTS

Being able to press, trap, sag, or play regular gives a start toward developing the multiple defense game. But there is even more that can be done without changing to zone or full court defense to multiply the defensive weaponry. For example, since some teams run their offense better to one side (oftentimes their right side) of the floor the entire defensive unit can adjust to overplay each man hard to the offense's better side in an effort to force the play to the less effective area. We once pulled a nice upset away from home because our films showed that this particular team functioned better when the offense moved down their left side. We forced the ball to the right by overplaying the left side of every man and by easing the pressure on men on the offensive right in order to encourage the ball to be thrown to points of least resistance. We practiced about twenty minutes on this the day before the game. This little extra effort on our part caused great confusion to the offense by breaking their rhythm. A little defensive twist can cause major offensive problems.

It may not be necessary or even wise to overplay an entire team. But nearly every game we play, whether we use man-to-man or zone, we instruct at least one of our players to overplay a particular opponent to the right or left, or toward the inside or outside. Opponents always have players who play best when allowed to do special things. Once these are identified, overplaying can bother that individual's effectiveness.

We occasionally overplay the opponent's guards hard on the inside to push them outside toward the forwards. This helps stop the guard's driving game. It is also effective in hampering the opponent's post man. When a guard's man does not possess the ball he can drop in easily from this inside position to help on the post man. Since he is getting help from the front, it allows our post defender to play a better rebound position game as well.

At some point in most games a particular opponent will develop a hot shooting hand. When this occurs the best defense is to keep the basketball out of his hands. By overplaying in his direction while his defender plays between him and the ball we are often able to keep him from handling the ball, at least in his most desired floor position. The same can be done to upset a team's best playmaker.

We have used our option to trap whenever the ball happened to go to a weak ballhandler or inexperienced man, or when it went to the corner, or into the post man. Once the team is aware of the many adjustments they can make easily and how they help produce victory, they will love to play this kind of game. It also makes the team feel good to look back on a victory and feel that a little overplay, or a shift in team defensive position may have caused just enough confusion to the opponent to produce the win. This kind of experience builds team confidence and defensive pride like nothing else can.

DEFENSIVE RECOVERIES

If a team plays a ball-pressure defense as we like to do they must be prepared to help out defenders who get beaten by the driver. Pressuring the ball heavily will cause the defender to be vulnerable to the drive. But this is superior to allowing good outside shooting or a fine passing attack to go unmolested. Once the open shot is taken there is no further defense possible for that particular shot. That is, if it hits the goal no amount of blocking out or anything else can help the defensive team. Almost the same is true if the offense is allowed to pass freely. They will soon find an open man close to the goal and the defense will be helpless to recover. However, by setting up a recovery system the defense can still redeem itself if a defender is beaten by a driver. For this reason we believe that ball pressure defense is the best kind possible. At its best it seriously upsets the shooting and passing. If the defense can execute recoveries well to help any defender beaten by a drive, the offense will really have to function well to score effectively.

There are four recoveries that we drill throughout the season. Recovering is essential to both the man-to-man and zone defenses so time is doubly well-spent practicing it. It involves the defensive unit in adjusting momentarily anytime one of the defenders is beaten by the ballhandler. The four recoveries are: guard for guard, forward for guard, guard for forward, and the deep-post recoveries.

The guard for guard recovery is illustrated in Diagram 4-10. Player 1 is beaten by the drive but his guard teammate moves obliquely backward to prevent the driver from going all the way. Player 2 would not lose visual contact with his own man. In this and in all recovery situations except the deep-post one, there are three possibilities that may result from the recovery move. (1) In most cases the original defender will be able to catch right up with his own man and the helping defender will slide back over to his own man as in Diagram 4-10. (2) If the driver keeps coming right into the recovery man, player 2 in this case, he will have to take him and player 1, the original defender on the ballhandler, will move across and exchange men. (Diagram 4-11.) (3) The guards might trap the ballhandler as in Diagram 4-12. If this occurs, the rest of the team should react to pick up the steal as players 4 and 5 have done in the diagram. It should be observed that in the three diagrams all five players flexed a bit when one defender was beaten so that if the recovery failed at the first point, someone else could at least prevent a lay-in. The good defensive unit will be ball-conscious in this manner.

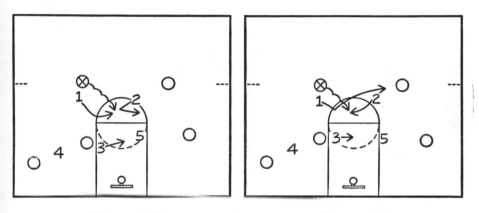

Diagram 4-10   Diagram 4-11

Diagrams 4-13 through 4-15 show the forward recovering for the guard. When the driver beats a guard to the outside a forward must help to recover him just as the other guard must do when the driver goes toward the inside. The only difference encountered in the forward recovery for the guard is that the forward must move back straight toward the goal more than obliquely. (Diagram 4-13.) If the forward moves up toward the ballhandler any more than a step, he will open his man for an easy cut to the goal and a lay-in.

If the forward will drop straight back two or three steps toward the goal quickly, the driver will usually pass off to the forward's man for a corner shot. This is better for the defense than what would have resulted otherwise. Again, the two defenders involved may switch men if the driver forces the forward to take him or they may also spring a trap. We have had many steals result when our forward had to stay with the driver and the guard came from behind to steal the pass to the forward in the corner. (Diagram 4-14.)

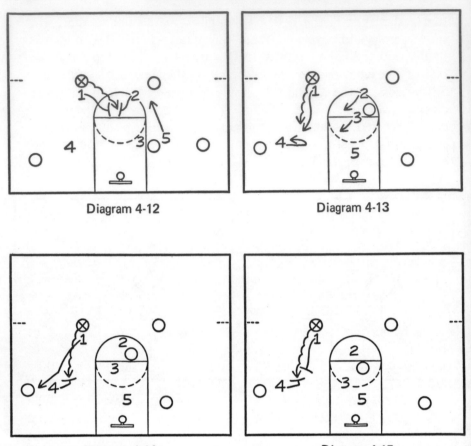

Diagram 4-12   Diagram 4-13

Diagram 4-14   Diagram 4-15

The guard recovery for the forward follows the same pattern. If the forward beats his defender with an inside drive, the defensive guard will try to slow down the ballhandler so that his man can recover. (Diagram 4-16.) The guard, player 1, must move back toward the goal to prevent the driver from going all the way. If the original defender catches back up, all is well. If not, the exchange or trap may result as in the other recoveries. (Diagrams 4-17 and 4-18.) In all recoveries it is wise to instruct the defender who drops off to help recover the driver, not to lunge at the man. This would make it more likely that the driver could beat both men, and it puts the helper too far from his own man to cover him if a pass goes to him. Diagrams 4-16 through 4-18 again illustrate how all five men must react when one man is beaten.

The most crucial of all the recoveries is the deep-post. (Diagram 4-19.) Anytime a defender is beaten to the base line side,

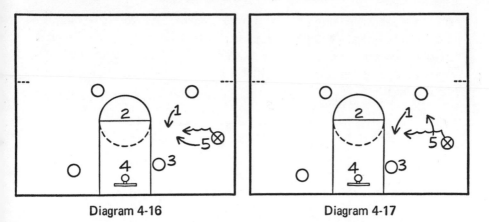

Diagram 4-16   Diagram 4-17

a recovery is the only chance to prevent the lay-in. There are two ways that the defense may recover in the deep-post. The preferred is to have the weakside forward stop the ball. (Diagram 4-19.) But occasionally the post man will be in a position where he will have to do it instead. (Diagram 4-20.) Regardless, the effort must be made. To fail to do so means a sure lay-in. It may result in a lay-in anyway but the offense will have to make a pass to get it and they could throw it away.

There are two differences in the deep-post recovery from the others. We *always* trap this play. We use no other option. The ball is down deep on the base line and it is difficult to pass out from this position. Since we always trap, the three remaining defenders must shift into the triangle stealing positions. In Diagram 4-19 the weak side guard, 2, picks up the weak side forward's man as the trap is set. If the post man has to trap, the weak side forward will

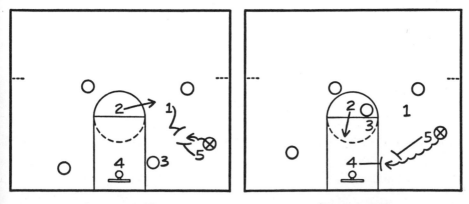

Diagram 4-18   Diagram 4-19

try to cover the man our post man leaves uncovered. (Diagram 4-20.) The guards will pick up passes thrown across under the goal to the forward or deep to the guards. If the ball escapes the trap, players must scramble to regain their original positions. (See Drill 13 in chapter 5.)

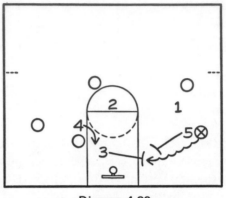

Diagram 4-20

When a team masters the recovery moves they are able to put on ball pressure without getting hurt very often. It takes some time for players to learn to watch both their man and the ball and to be able to anticipate traps and recoveries. When the team finally captures it they are able to convert what for a moment would appear to be a good offensive break-through into no advantage. In fact, the team will often turn the tables and put the offense into a real disadvantage. In one instance the driver will be driving toward an apparent hole and in the next find himself bound up in a firm trap. This kind of play can change the momentum of a game.

SOME REMINDERS FOR MAN-TO-MAN DEFENSE

Although this book is not a catalog of every point of defense, we would like to share a list of defensive reminders we issue to our players which serve as a refresher to them. The list covers many of the points we emphasize on defense. We have no magic total number of these; we add as we go along each season.

Defensive Reminders

There are different ways to play different teams and

individuals. Every player must learn each way and we will drill on these so we can perform the job. Following are some ways of playing individual defense:

Straight-away—keep between your man and the bucket and concentrate on the shooting shoulder.

Overplaying the inside—this type overplays any cut or drive so as to force the offense to go to the outside. The reverse is used occasionally, forcing the offense inside. To *overplay* place your body so it is partly in the path you do not want him to go.

Overplaying the strong hand—overplay the right hand of a right-handed boy, for example.

Overplaying opposite the pivot foot—overplay the free foot; the player can drive quicker in that direction. To go the other way he has to cross-step.

Stance—Use the boxer stance with one foot slightly forward; feet should be as wide apart as possible and still allow good movement; weight backward but evenly distributed on your feet; head up; back straight; arms spread with the one raised which is on the same side as the foot which is forward.

Specifics:

1. Keep the body *low* out on the floor and move the legs with force. Use your arms to help you move faster and to keep balance. You have to keep low out on the floor to be a good defender. Straighten up as your player nears the goal.
2. Spread the legs as far as they will go and still be moved quickly when guarding outside.
3. Commit no unneeded fouls. Instead work to draw the offensive foul, the best move in basketball.
4. Move your back foot first when your man cuts or drives and keep in front of him. Keep your weight on the front foot so you can push off backward or sideways.
5. Never lose sight of your man. If you must choose between seeing your man or the ball, watch the man.
6. Play the ball tight, force the man out. Make him turn his back.
7. If your man is one pass from the ball, watch him closely; be in front of any man underneath the goal.
8. If your man is two passes away, sag off and turn so that you can see the man and the ball by looking at a point halfway between the two. Also station the body so that you can get in front of your man if he cuts to the ball.
9. Try to avoid switching by going over the top of the screen (between your man and the screen). Overplaying the cut toward the ball will aid in this. If you do get picked off, switch and take the man who screened you. Call it out, even though it's automatic.

10. Talk on defense.

11. Try not to cross the feet. Keep a wide base. But the main thing is to keep your body in front of your man, even if you do cross your feet.

12. Keep one hand chest high as your man moves. Make the offense run into it.

13. When playing beside a man, keep one forearm on his back with the hand sticking above his shoulder. Do not simply lay your hand on him. Put the other arm between the man and the ball.

14. Keep in front of all cutters and drivers. Make them take the long way. Force them to go a way they do not want to go. *Pressure the cutter.*

15. Overplay the opponent's strong points. Make him do something else.

16. Overplay forwards especially. Force them to go the way you want. Since most offenses start on the wings, push them out.

17. On the drive defense, drop your outside arm and turn the body toward the driver. Make the driver hit your outside shoulder for the offensive foul.

18. Do not reach in or slap on defense. Move your body.

19. Do not try to block too many shots. Hump the back when you try and keep the hand high.

20. Use your feeler hand when moving with your man. Stick out the hand in the direction you are moving as you guard a dribbler or cutter.

21. Prevent the good pass. A lob is anybody's ball. Try to deflect every pass; one of your teammates may pick it off. Pressure every inside pass.

22. When you trap a man, never foul. He is in trouble, do not help him.

23. Get back fast on defense or sit down. Make a defensive fast break. This is mandatory.

24. *Never* give fast break lay-ins. If you can't move faster without the ball than they do with it, you are in the wrong game.

25. Trap a player when he is already guarded closely by one man and either (a) he is off-balance; (b) he drives into a second defender; (c) he turns his back to you; (d) his teammates have cleared and left him at full court with no place to throw but forward; (e) on crosses or screens occasionally. Most often these are very safe out on the floor. At times they are okay even within twenty feet of the goal, if you don't over-use it; or (f) in the corner occasionally. But you should be able to get the ballhandler to effect the trap by making no more than *three quick steps*. If you have to run farther than this, he will throw over you as you approach.

26. You must *go to the ball* on every rebound or loose ball. Go to the ball is the name of the game.

27. Try to defend you man's shooting shoulder.

28. *Manos Arriba!* Keep those hands up. Make defense a challenge to your own courage and ability.
29. Beat your man to his chosen spot on the floor.

By doing this you will be able to play better defense and will be fifty percent more valuable to your team. In the big ball games, the ones you have to win, defense will carry you to victory.

5

Drills for Teaching
Man-to-Man Defenses

1. Reaction Drills

    a.   Mass movement of players, following coach's directions (right, left, oblique, etc.). Players take only two steps each time.

    b.   Players play 1-on-1 step for step. Two players face each other. Player 1 makes only two or three quick steps. Player 2 tries to match those steps. Then change after twenty or thirty seconds.

    c.   Hand movement drill. Same drill as in 1b., but with players matching the hand movement instead of foot movement.

2. Body Position

    a.   Mass drill—movement on coach's directions. Emphasize proper stance.

    b.   Partners face each other and roll ball back and forth as they shuffle-step laterally down the floor.

    c.   One-on-one to emphasize position, pressuring the ball, overplaying, etc.

3. Footwork

    a.   Backward running, length of floor.

    b.   Full court trail. (Diagram 5-1.)

c. Triangle footwork in defensive stance. (Diagram 5-2.) Do *twice, reverse.* Repeat as long as desired.

d. Rope jump

e. Square jumping—two footed. (Diagram 5-3.)

f. Dot the "i" jump. One broad jump, one jump for height.

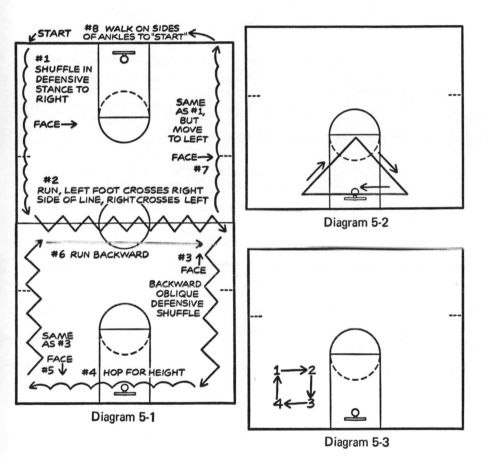

Diagram 5-2

Diagram 5-1

Diagram 5-3

4. Hands and Arms

a. Hand position drills—start ballhandler in back court and have defender guard with hands out and palms up. Do not allow a steal. As the ballhandler gradually gets into scoring range, the hand is raised. Have the dribbler stop about twenty feet from goal. Then the defense crowds up, both hands up to force a bad pass. The passer tries to pass to a new player through the defender, who tries to get a fingertip on the ball to deflect it.

b. Standard man in passing circle, or "bull in the ring" drill trying to deflect passes.

c. Three-man keep away in a limited area. The object is to deflect a pass.

5. Guarding the Various Positions.

Have all players play one-on-one at the guard, forward, and post spots. Each player should be able to defend at all spots. Get tight on the ballhandler.

6. Position Drills for Guard, Forward, Post

a. Guard positioning—after three to five passes in which the defense shifts positions, as from Diagrams 5-4 to 5-7, and back each time, the offense will try to score.

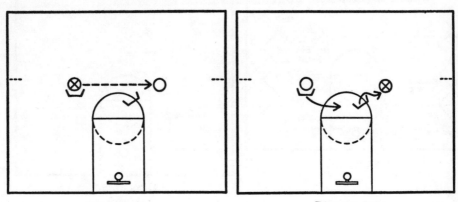

Diagram 5-4   Diagram 5-5

b. Guard-forward positioning—same rules as in 6a. (Diagrams 5-8 to 5-11.)

c. Guards and forwards—same as in 6b, but add the other guard. Use regular and press positions. (Diagram 5-12.)

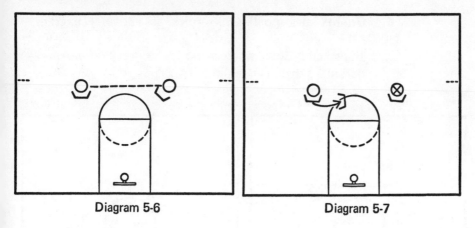

Diagram 5-6

Diagram 5-7

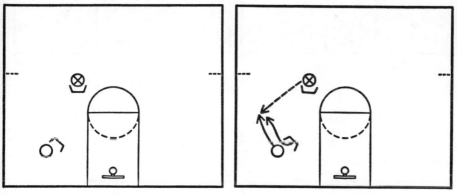

Diagram 5-8

Diagram 5-9

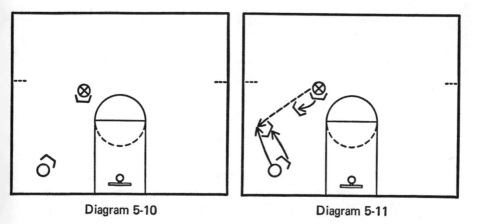

Diagram 5-10

Diagram 5-11

d.   Guards and post—same rules as above. (Diagram 5-13.)

e.   High and low post—same rules—very *important* defensive drill. (Diagram 5-14.)

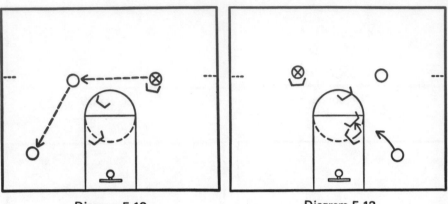

Diagram 5-12   Diagram 5-13

f.   Guard-forward and post—same rules as above. (Diagram 5-15.)

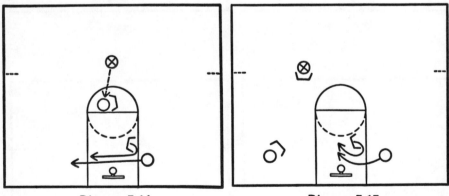

Diagram 5-14   Diagram 5-15

Then add four- and five-man drills to cover positioning. Make three to five passes to force concentration on positioning in the regular and press defenses before allowing a shot. Drill sag positions and trapping in the same way as the season progresses.

g.   Work 1–1 at all positions using the various over-plays at guard and forward.

7. Guarding the Post Area and the Driver

    a.   One-on-one play being sure to have players use proper hand and body position out on floor. They must straighten up as the offense gets nearer the goal.

    b.   One-on-one cut-off drill. Player 1 starts behind the ballhandler and must beat him to a spot and cut him off. He does not pace alongside the ballhandler. (Diagram 5-16.)

    c.   Drawing the offensive foul. The defense must drop his outside arm, but turn his outside shoulder right toward the driver so as to prevent the driver's head and shoulders passing him. (Diagram 5-17.)

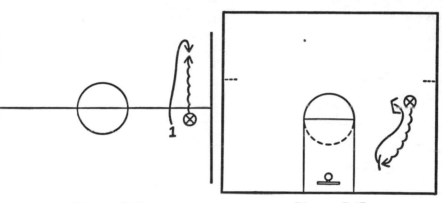

Diagram 5-16   Diagram 5-17

8. Cutter Defense

    a.   The backdoor cut. The defense turns with the cutter so as to keep sight of his man. (Diagram 5-18.)

    b.   A one-on-one drill in which the offense makes the 6 moves in sequence as in Diagram 5-19 while the defender matches his steps as in Diagram 5-20. The coach has a ball at the guard position. This teaches going from one pass away defense, to post defense, to two passes away. Repeat from the other wing.

    c.   Give and go defense. (Diagram 5-21.)

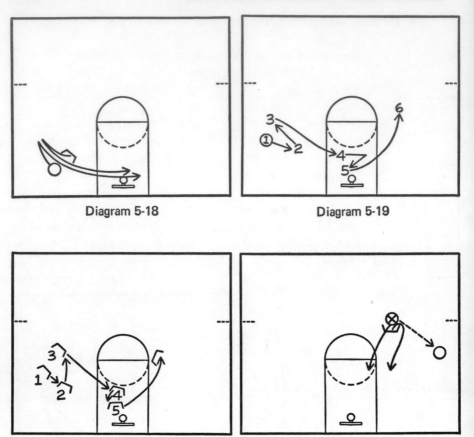

Diagram 5-18

Diagram 5-19

Diagram 5-20

Diagram 5-21

    d.   Lane cutter defense. (Diagram 5-22.)

    e.   Lane cutter defense. (Diagram 5-23.)

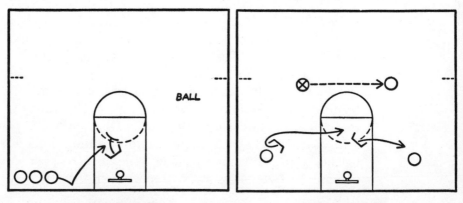

Diagram 5-22

Diagram 5-23

9. Defense Against the Screens

    a.   Playing over the top. (Diagrams 5-24 & 5-25.)

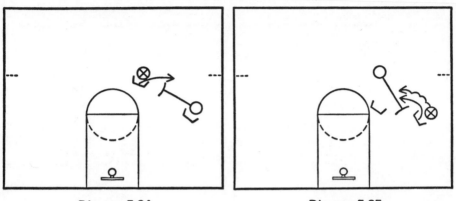

Diagram 5-24   Diagram 5-25

    b.   Post-forward screens. (Diagram 5-26.)
    c.   Shuffle cut—same rules as above. (Diagram 5-27.)

Diagram 5-26   Diagram 5-27

    d.   Screen and roll—use the switch on this close-range screen. (Diagram 5-28.)
    e.   Go through or behind out on floor—no switch unless your rules are to switch on this. (Diagram 5-29.)
    f.   Post split. Drop back and switch on the guard-guard split. (Diagram 5-30.) On guard-forward split you

must be able to overplay the cuts and avoid the switch if possible. If you are rubbed off the post, a switch must be used, the post man switching to whomever is given the ball. (Diagram 5-31.)

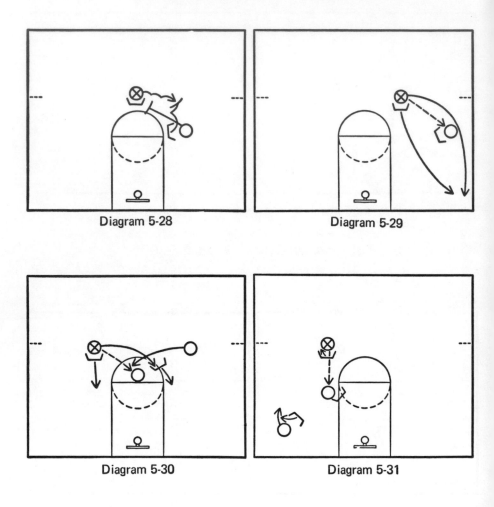

Diagram 5-28

Diagram 5-29

Diagram 5-30

Diagram 5-31

g.   Clear drill. (Diagram 5-32.)

10. Team Defense Drills

Much half-court 5-on-5 must be worked to drill the positioning and movement of the specific defense used. The individual drills and two or three-man drills are helpful in formulating habits, but more time must gradually be put in on five against five. (Very important.) We allow the offense the ball a specific period of time, or number of possessions, or scores and try to get a concentrated defensive effort. We then turn the ball over to the defense so the first offensive team can compete against what the first defensive team did in terms of points yielded.

It is good to make the offense pass the ball a set number of times at the start of the drill in order to drill positioning and slides. The same is true of man-to-man, zone, or press team defense. Games can be worked up to give the defense certain points for steals, jump balls, rebounds, deflections, etc., to emphasize what you are teaching.

11. Passing Drills

Passing drills to help get laning across are helpful. Some of these are:
    a.   The six-point drill. (See Drill 8b.)
    b.   Triangle passing. The offense can move two steps either direction to get open. (Diagram 5-33.)

Diagram 5-32   Diagram 5-33

    c.   Three-man keep away. Man without the ball can move two or three steps either direction. (Diagram 5-34.)

12. Trapping

See chapter 13 for working 5-on-5, then add the trap moves.

It is best to drill the two, three, and four-man drills before using 5-on-5. Some of these drills are:

    a.   Trap without fouling—emphasize proper trap techniques. (Diagram 5-35.)

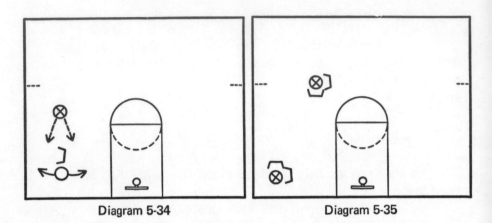

Diagram 5-34   Diagram 5-35

    b.   Anticipation move—Players 1 and 2 try to anticipate the pass from the trap and steal it. (Diagram 5-36.)

    c.   The trap keys—drill all the keys for trapping. (Diagram 5-37.)
       (1) deep post trap
       (2) ballhandler turns back
       (3) ballhandler off-balance
       (4) ball stuck in corner
       (5) ballhandler deserted on the clear

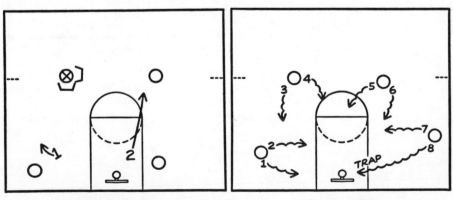

Diagram 5-36   Diagram 5-37

      (6) screen and roll

      (7) dribbler drives into a second defender

Make these 2-on-2, then add the 3 and 4 men on defense for the steal.

     d.   Drill all the types of traps 5-on-5.

        (1) guard-guard

        (2) guard-forward

        (3) forward-guard

        (4) deep post

Be sure to work *recovering* if the trap is beaten by scrambling back into positions.

     e.   Stop the dribble and get into the lanes. Work 5-on-5. One player dribbles. When he stops, all the defense moves up into the pass lanes to steal the pass.

13. Recoveries

Start the ball in the left corner and allow the four guards and forwards to alternate in beating the defender. The left forward will drive to his right and be recovered. Then he will throw the ball back out, will receive it again, and be allowed to drive inside to his left. The process is repeated with each offensive player driving inside of his defender first to the right, then to the left. This way each recovery is practiced. The whole process can be reversed by coming back around from the right corner.

PART TWO

ZONE DEFENSES

6

Ruling the Zone Defenses

Anyone who can play good man-to-man defense can become a good zone player; however, there are some differences in playing the two types. A player cannot be at his best in a zone unless he knows the special individual techniques zones require and rules to cover the offensive situations he will be forced to defend. There are not so many points of variance to make teaching good zone defense prohibitive; but, if few in number, they are crucial. Most of these points of variance will apply to every zone style, fortunately. The only pertinent differences between zones would occur when a team goes from a containing style of zone to a laning or pressing zone. Chapters 7 and 8 deal with these styles, respectively, and will point out what differences exist. Right now we will give only light reference to those two team styles as we point up the more specific essentials to successful individual zone play.

BODY AND FLOOR POSITION

The zone player can and should pressure the ball very hard in the scoring area. He can afford to scoot right up under the ballhandler and get a good wide base because the rest of the defense is even more ball-conscious than when playing the man-to-man. We insist that our players be ball-conscious in every defense, of course, but the zone is more conducive to this than the man-to-man. The other four defensive men must be able to recover for the defender pressuring the ballhandler. When the zone permits outside shots, they should at least be hurried. Defending closely with a wide base while using the hands to intimidate the shooter-passer will increase the zone team's effectiveness.

The same two stances as discussed for the man-to-man, open and closed, may apply to the zone defender. We *prefer* the *open* stance for zones, however, except in the post area. We do this for three reasons. (1) The open stance allows the entire defense to see the ball better because their bodies are open toward the ball. (2) This stance permits the defense to have one hand pointing into the vital lane area where we do not want the ball to go, while the other hand can extend toward the nearest outside offensive player. (3) The normal danger involved in using the open stance in man-to-man defense is that an offensive man can backdoor cut the defense more easily than when the closed stance is used. But this risk is reduced in zone play because the back defenders should be more ready to help out a beaten defender because they are zoning. Still, when the defense wants to play to shut the ball off a player, or when guarding the post, the closed stance is better. It boils down to the facts that defenders can watch one man better in a closed stance, but will be able to see the ball better and to help teammates out more with the open stance. The wise coach will teach the stance or stances that help accomplish what he deems to be of more importance to his defense.

Floor position is very important in zone play. Once the specific area that the team is to defend is determined, all players should keep floor position in that area as a unit. A common zone mistake is to allow one player to go out on his own to pressure the ball or attempt to steal while the rest of the defense plays another style of game. One over-eager man can hurt his team's defense by extending himself unduly, allowing the ballhandler to split into a defense that is stretched too far in one area to make a good recovery. Too much free lancing like this can be a serious mistake. Failing to keep floor balance has sent a lot of teams back to a man-to-man.

A zone team must be well-drilled in recovering or helping out on defense, especially if they pressure the ball correctly. In helping out on defense the individual should drop off the nearest offensive man *as far as he can* when this man is two passes from the ball and still be able to get right on him just as quickly as the ball can get to him. It is important that players push themselves on this point. It is easy for a man to cheat his teammates on this. He must try to get right into the *middle of the defense* as much as possible to be a good team man. Of course, the defender can reach his outside man quickly if he drops only a step from him. But he will not help his mates this way. Still, he must get to the ball in time to prevent a clear shot or easy pass; therefore, each player will have to gauge his distance according to his quickness. It will be that maximum distance he can cover if he really slides hard in and out. (Drill 7 in chapter 11.)

Because of our emphasis on watching the ball, talking is one of the most essential elements in tough zone play, even more so than in the man-to-man. Men who are on the back line or men who find themselves on the weak side two passes from the ball are in a great position to help their teammates out vocally and must make the effort. A great zone cannot be a silent one.

Post Play

Post play is very crucial in any zone defense. Although some formations (2–1–2, 1–3–1, 2–3) expect primarily one man to defend the post area, there are times in every zone when a second or even a third player must cover for him, either as a matter of course or in an emergency situation. More time need be spent on post play than any other single factor in zone defense. The post man not only must defend the man in the middle of the offense but also keep in mind his responsibility to help *protect the basket.* To do that he has to know what is going on behind him. Furthermore, many offenses keep rotating players in and out of the middle so the post man must be able to pick up each new cutter who enters his area. A boy who is flat-footed or who does not keep *turning his head* to see what is going on to either side and to his rear will be a poor post defender. Even a good athlete who may be trying his best to see in all directions must depend on his teammates to talk constantly to him to let him know of cutters or screeners. (See Drills 1j and 8 in chapter 11.)

Complicating the post man's task is the fact that most coaches will try to get the ball to the post as often as possible as they attack zones. Thus, it takes a good athlete to defend the post area and it helps to have two or three good ones.

SPECIFIC RULES FOR THE ZONE DEFENSES

The general zone responsibilities regarding body and floor

position with tough post play are basic factors for a successful zone. Add now to this the ability to master the following listing of specific responsibilities and it will determine how successful a zone team can be. The team that learns these rules will be able to respond to nearly any offensive pattern they will encounter. Further, they will be able to adjust into any zone alignment with much more ease than could a team without these habits. Once these rules are drilled and learned the coach needs to teach only the specific slides he wants in the zone defensive alignment he wants to use. The players will be able to do the rest.

1. *The cut to the goal.* When an offensive player cuts, the defender in his area must go with him two or three steps toward the free throw lane. He should call loudly, "cutter." The defender will stay in the lane area to jam up the middle until a new offensive player moves into his area. The cutter will be absorbed by the rest of the defense. The reason for going two or three steps is to prevent the quick give and go pass. (Diagram 6-1.) Another possibility occasionally employed is to allow the front defender to go through with the first *guard* cutter. (Diagram 6-2.) He may stay man-to-man with him or he may just rotate with the other front man as soon as the cutter goes through the lane, or even to the corner where a back man would cover. (See Drills 1f and 9a in chapter 11.)

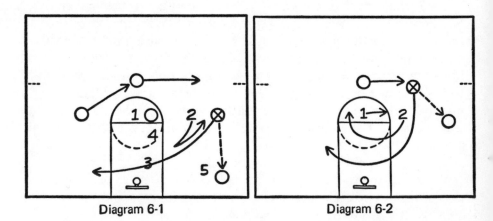

Diagram 6-1   Diagram 6-2

2. *The driver toward the goal.* It is important to try to stay one-on-one with the driver when possible; assume individual responsibility. If he is able to draw extra defenders toward

him, he can pass off and hurt the defense. Exceptions would be when a driver can be forced into a trap situation as part of the defense, for example the deep post trap. Otherwise, do your *best* to *prevent* a man from penetrating the defense with the ball. Keep the ball away from the inside. (See Drill 1g in chapter 11.)

3. *The baseline screen.* There are two places that zone teams will face screening tactics—on the baseline and out on the floor. When a screen is set on the baseline defender, he must immediately step *over the top* of the screen, face out toward the front, and keep his hand nearest the goal right in front of the screener. *Two* steps up and *one* over will accomplish this. He gets set to cover the cutter coming around the screen, but cannot afford to leave the screener entirely alone until another backline defender tells him to do so, or else the screener himself will be wide open. Player 5 must keep his inside hand on the screener until he gets help to prevent the pass to this man in lay-in position. (Diagram 6-3.) Five could jump out on the cutter too soon and allow an easy pass to the screener. (See Drill 9c in chapter 11.)

4. *The outside screens.* The man being screened again must take two quick steps frontward and one over just as the screen is set. (Diagram 6-4.) By doing this immediately he is able to force the offense either to go out very wide or to reverse direction. These screen rules are most important. (See Drill 9e in chapter 11.)

5. *Ball in the high post.* When the ball is successfully thrown into the high post, the post defender tightens right up on him.

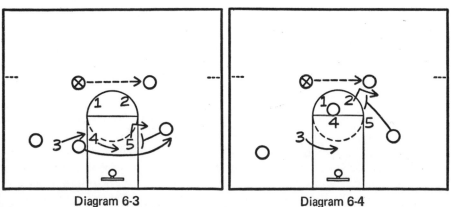

Diagram 6-3   Diagram 6-4

The front man or men squeeze in from in front and the other back men move to cover the deep post goal area. (Diagram 6-5.) The ball must be forced out. The shot or pass under must be prevented, if possible. (See Drills 1j, 8, and 9i in chapter 11.)

6. *Ball into the low post.* All players must try to smother or umbrella the ball if it is thrown into this area. It is better to allow any other shot than this one.

7 *The deep post recovery or trap.* Whenever a driver beats the defense on the baseline, the opposite weak side man must move across the lane to draw the offensive foul or to trap. (Diagram 6-6.) The weak side guard drops to cover for the back man.

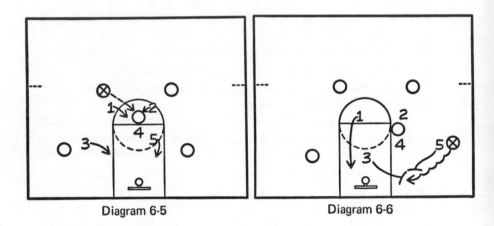

Diagram 6-5   Diagram 6-6

8. *The baseline rover and tandem.* When using a point (one-front) defense such as 1–2–2 and 1–3–1, or when matching up on defense, a rover rule is needed. The deep post defender may have to go man-to-man with the rover when the offense is in set position. In the 1–2–2 the two back men may have to tandem against a 1–3–1 offense that is effective along the baseline. Whenever the ball is stopped out front, the low man would stay with the rover. (Diagram 6-7.) The same idea can be applied in matching zone defenses against a rover. For example, in a 2–3 match-up the back man on the strong side (the side rotated toward) would rove the base when necessary. (Diagram 6-8.) (See Drill 9h in chapter 11.)

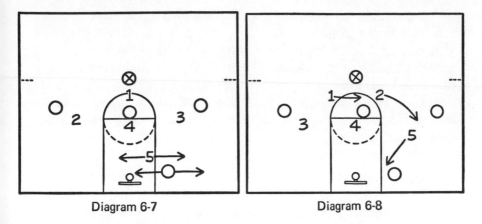

Diagram 6-7   Diagram 6-8

9. *Emergency corner coverage.* Every now and then a back man will cover a wing area and an offensive man will be open in the corner on his side. While the "rover" rule prevents this in most instances, it will happen. Emergency corner coverage is simply this: whenever the *middle man must move to cover a corner man, he does.* The weak side back man then moves into the post area and the weak side guard drops to cover the weak side rebound area. Diagram 6-9 shows 4 covering the right corner. Player 3 jams into the middle and 1 covers the weak side goal area. If the ball is reversed back around the horn, the players scramble to get back into normal positions. Drilling this occasionally will teach the habit. In our discussion of match-up rules, we cover this with our "deep corner cut" rule.

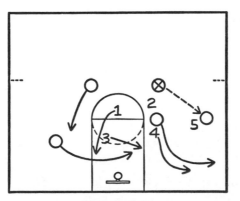

Diagram 6-9

Being able to excute these rules will help a team become effective in the zone defense. There are a few other simple rules that are applicable to the matching zone defense that will be explained in chapter 9 which are specifically for that style of zone; however they happen to make pretty good sense to the regular zones as well and do not contradict the above rules. Next to outright hustle, a working knowledge of zone rules is a zone team's most important possession.

Drilling the Rules

The best way to drill these rules is to go over them several times in 5-on-5 half-court situations. The coach can take one-third or one-half of the rules each day and drill them separately and repeatedly several times. The following practice he can work on the remaining rules. Each move offers itself as a drill. (See Drills in chapter 11, which cover each zone fundamental.)

Trapping

It is not necessary to repeat trapping methods here because the half-court traps are all alike as noted before. The same basic man-to-man traps as were detailed in chapter 3 apply to zone trapping as well. The coach can use the four traps as he sees fit in any zone: the guard-to-guard, the guard-to-forward, forward-to-guard, and the deep-post. When a team learns how and when to trap they can use it with any defensive type or style. (See Drill 9g in chapter 11.)

Giving a list of the specific zone rules to the players to read has helped our teaching zone defense. We give a sheet out a day or two in advance of the practice at which we plan to begin teaching the zone rules. Doing this with zone rules and other items has helped us teach better and quicker. When the players know these rules well enough to execute them, they can play a lot of zone defense. Becoming multiple with zones is made that much easier.

TIPS ON INDIVIDUAL ZONE PLAY

1. Never guard space—fall into the defense and help.
2. Pressure the ball in the scoring area.

3. Do not have two men on the ball unless it is a trap.
4. Back men must work together and must turn their heads constantly to see the action behind them.
5. Keep the ball out of the inside area.
6. Talk, talk, talk.
7. Slide hard *into* the defense and *back out* to the ball.
8. Cover the weak side rebound.
   (The drills listed under Drill 1 in chapter 11 cover these tips.)

The zone rules for individuals are specifics that a player would not know on his own. These principles must be taught on top of the solid man-to-man foundation. Fortunately all of these rules are logical and do not require the teaching time one might assume. A word of warning for all coaches is simply this: unless you are willing to take the time to cover the zone rules described in this chapter, do not plan to use the zone very often. Use it only as a change-up for a brief period. If you expect to depend much on a zone or zones, to neglect teaching all these rules is defensive suicide.

7

Coaching the
Containing Zone Defenses

The containing zones are labeled as such because they defend basically the prime percentage scoring area with emphasis on players who are not guarding the ball to sag in to contain the free throw and basket area. The ball will be pressured in the scoring area and the man defending the ballhandler must get right on the ballhandler. Although some coaches do not try to put on a lot of ball pressure while using the zone, it is generally conceded that, given today's fine shooters, this pressure is necessary. The zone defender can take more chances by pressuring hard than in man-to-man since the rest of the zone defense is even more alive to help recover for him. Therefore, the defender can spread wide and really attack the ballhandler. We like for our players to do this. The defender tries to prevent the shot and must use his hands freely to discourage passes to the inside. He still will work to prevent most drives but can afford to allow them occasionally rather than to give up pressuring the ball.

FLOOR POSITIONS FOR CONTAINING ZONES

Players one pass from the ball except post men should open up toward the ball and shift toward the middle. Both hands should be spread; the inside hand should point to the post area, the other toward the nearest open man on the outside. (Diagrams 7-1 and 7-2.) It is important to be pressuring the middle area as suggested in the zone rules in chapter 6.

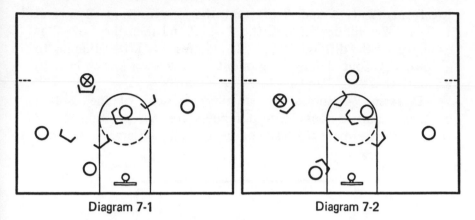

Diagram 7-1   Diagram 7-2

Forward or wing men should close their stance when guarding anyone in the post area but open up as their man moves outside of close range. We want to keep the ball outside. In the containing zone they should be careful not to push too far out on the floor and extend the defense too much. They must prevent passes up to seventeen or twenty feet, but cannot spread themselves too thin and allow the offense to penetrate the defense. The whole idea is to keep the ball on the outside. We refer to this defense as our "20 feet defense," since we seldom allow anyone to take himself past that range in this defense.

The defensive post man can play back behind the high post and cover the goal well since the front men are able to help keep the ball out of that area. The post man will front any offensive man in the deep post area as always. If a man gets the ball anywhere in the post area, the post defender really pressures him hard. He must try to keep him from shooting or passing underneath. He tries desperately to get him to turn his back on the goal area and get rid of the ball. The guards should remember their rule to help apply pressure to make him give up the ball.

Players defending *two passes* from the ball must sag deep into the keyhole area. This is fundamental help-side defense. But zone defenders must be very adept at this and have to keep aware of any cutters who may be moving behind them into open zone spots.

TWO-FRONT CONTAINING ZONES

The two basic frontal attacks for zone defenses are the

two-front (2–1–2 and 2–3) and the one-front (1–2–2 and 1–3–1). We will discuss first the 2–1–2 and then the 1–2–2 as examples of the different fronts. It requires very little adjusting to go into any zone defense alignment when a team knows how to use both the 2–1–2 and 1–2–2.

Diagram 7-3 shows the starting positions of the 2–1–2 containing zone defense. The defenders are in a position to put good pressure around the basket area, one may observe.

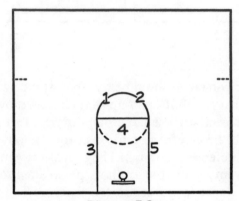

Diagram 7-3

Slides of the Front Men

Diagrams 7-4 through 7-11 show how the front men move to cover their areas. They cover the *point* and *wing* while containing the post area. The defense will have to defend against both the one and two-front offenses since offensive teams will vary in their method of attacking the 2–1–2. Diagram 7-4 shows the defense against a two-front offense. The guard nearest the ball, player 1, takes the ballhandler at the *fringe* of the scoring area, not sooner. Player 2 drops back slightly and opens up extending one hand into the lane to pressure the post and the other toward the outside man nearest him as he watches the ball and keeps tabs on action both behind and in front of him.

Diagram 7-5 shows the defense facing a point offense such as a 1–3–1 which is a common attack against the 2–1–2. The front men must be able to alternate challenging the ballhandler when facing the one-front offenses depending on which side the offense is overloaded. The two men must talk to each other in order to alternate and cover toward the overloaded area. The guard farthest from the overload must challenge the ball. This pushes the other guard in the direction of the offensive overload. The ball must be challenged every time or the point man will drive freely right into the vulnerable middle area where the ball should not be allowed. Diagram 7-5 shows player 2 challenging the ballhandler. He must keep his *hands up* and pressure the side of the ballhandler nearest him. Using the hands to slow the passing is very crucial. He wants to push the ball away from his area or at least to force a lob pass if the ball does go over his head in the direction from which 2 came.

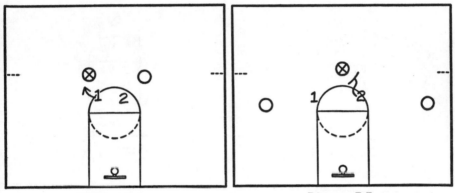

Diagram 7-4   Diagram 7-5

If the pass goes over 2's head, he must turn and chase the ball right away. Obviously, if a great shooter is on the wing 2 has deserted he can get a lot of shots, unless the back man on that side stops him, as he must do to make the defense go. If the ball is passed to the wing man on player 1's side, it leaves both 1 and 2 in good position. Diagrams 7-6 and 7-7 show the other basic guard slides. When the ball goes to the corner the front men sag to stop up the foul line area. (Diagram 7-6.)

When the ball goes into the post area both front men turn to try to force the ball out of the middle. (Diagram 7-7.) In the containing defenses remember that the front men both try to keep the ball from going into the middle as much as possible. This is the main point of this style of zone. If the ball is passed around the horn, the guards must chase the ball from the foul line extended area on both sides and must *avoid* the temptation of going into the corner, extending themselves too far. The guards should be aware that if the offense starts to pass the ball too rapidly from wing to point to wing and back that they cannot keep pace with the ball without adjusting. That adjustment is to move up slightly and get a hand in the pass lane from the point to the wing as the ball reverses in order to slow the pass down. When this becomes necessary the post man will have to move up slightly to help defend the middle, since it will be more vulnerable.

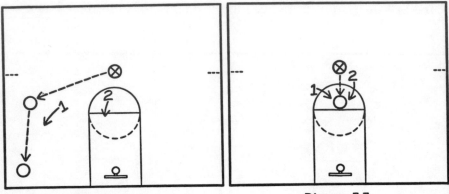

Diagram 7-6   Diagram 7-7

Variations of the Front Men's Slides

1. The two men can *tandem* as the ball comes down when the offense consistently shows a one-front offense. (Diagram 7-8.) Player 2 goes the direction of the first pass and 1 drops back to the foul line.

2. When the ball is being passed too rapidly around the outside to allow the guards to keep up, the pass lane from the corner to the wing should be cut off. (Diagram 7-9.) Player 1 gets into the pass lane from the corner to shut that pass off or slow it down. (Very important.)

3 The guards can occasionally alternate containing with laning the pass lanes to the wings. When this happens, the *post must* move up high to lane the post position, too. These laning techniques are discussed in the next chapter.

Slides of the Back Men

Slides of the forwards or back men, 4 and 5, are shown in

Diagrams 7-10 and 7-11. The forward on the *ball side* will cover the wing on his side up to the foul line extended, no further normally, and his corner. (Diagram 7-10.) Diagram 7-11 shows how 5 covers both the ball-side wing and corner. He must go to the ballhandler overplaying the *baseline* side with his hands up. This helps discourage any passing down low or to the corner. He will drop off the wing just as the front defender on his side, 2, nears the wing. (See Drill 2b in chapter 11.)

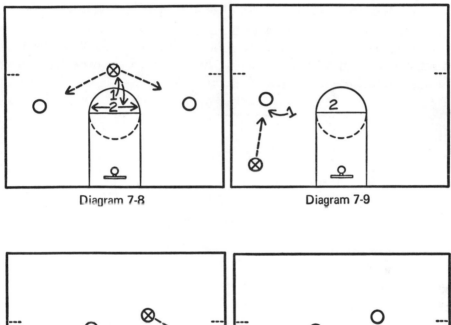

Diagram 7-8

Diagram 7-9

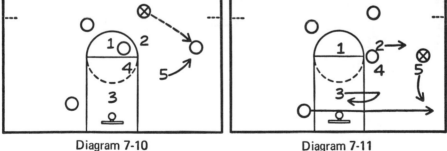

Diagram 7-10

Diagram 7-11

The back man on the side *opposite the ball* must cover the low post area as player 3 does in Diagrams 7-10 and 7-11. This is especially true when the middle man, 4, is playing high for any reason. In addition he may on rare occasions have to go into the high post if 4 pulls out to help 5 in an emergency. Again, he may also find himself having to go further to the corner the ball is in as an emergency measure but not if 2 and 5 are moving properly on the wing. But if it occurs that the weak side forward leaves his normal area to defend the high post or the ball side corner, the front man on his side must drop to the goal to cover for him. (Diagram 7-12.)

Basically the duties of the back men are to defend the wing on the ball side if a front man does not already have it covered and to cover the corner. The back man must be alive to cover the wing particularly fast when the front man on his side challenges the offensive point man as mentioned before. Otherwise, the front men can cover the wings easily enough, allowing the ball-side back men to protect the corner only. The back man opposite the ball must protect the low post basket area.

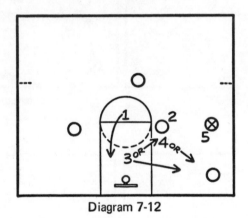

Diagram 7-12

Variations in Forward-Post Slides

Anytime the post must pull out to cover a man in the corner, which is hopefully not very often, the team may use a rotation with the ball-side back man and the post. (Diagram 7-13.) It is possible to set up rotations involving all three back men. As in Diagram 7-14, if player 3 moves to cover the far corner, 5 and 4 rotate to cover for him.

Post Play

The post man in the 2–1–2 is usually a player the coach

wants to keep in the free throw lane area. The 2—1—2 helps allow this because each forward or back man is expected to cover his respective wing area *and* corner. As said before, if the post *has to* go to a corner to prevent two points, he does. But that move is not one the team wants to use. If the ball-side forward is playing the back position correctly by using his hands and playing the pass lane and his front teammate comes to the wing *every* time, he can cover the corner well. (See Drill 8 in chapter 11.) The post area is the post man's prime responsibility so he must do his job there or the whole defense will fail. The post man tries to keep in front of any low post player. He must keep turning his head and be aware of any cutters into the post. He will *not* front at the foul lane area in the containing defense. He will play back as far as he can to protect the goal area because the guards out front are to work hard to keep the ball out of the high post. If the ball goes into the post the post defender must pressure the man immediately. If the offense begins to hurt the defense by working the ball to the post too much, or if the guards move higher into the lanes, the post man must move up. This makes the two forwards have to be more goal and low post conscious. Since the post man seldom fronts on defense he must do a good rebounding job.

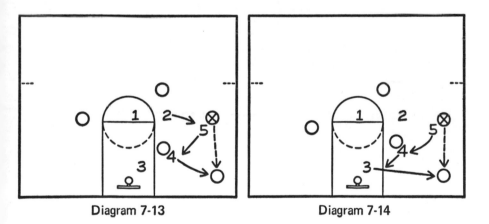

Diagram 7-13   Diagram 7-14

THE 2—3 CONTAINING ZONE DEFENSE

The 2—3 zone is much like the 2—1—2 and many coaches regard them as the same defense. But there is a basic difference between the two in the movement of the back-line players. All the information and variations can be adapted from the 2—1—2 to the 2—3 regarding the front men, back men, post, and rotations except for the following basic difference: the back men cover the wings and stay there which allows the guards to cover less area. The post pulls to the corner to cover any man there as a *normal* move, not an emergency one. The weak side back man goes to the post and the guard drops back. Diagram 7-15 shows the 2—3 slides.

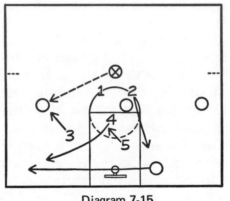

Diagram 7-15

Player 1 stops the ball. As it is thrown over him, 3 is ready to cover the wing. 4 moves to cover the corner and players 5 and 2 slide to cover the high and low post areas. If the ball were reversed back around the other way, the players would get back into their starting positions unless the coach chose to use a two, three or five man rotation.

THE ONE-FRONT CONTAINING ZONE DEFENSES

Point Man

The 1—2—2 positions are shown in Diagram 7-16. Player 1, the point man, is a key man in this defense. A good athlete in this position goes a long way toward making the defense work. For two years we had an outstanding boy in this spot when we played this style of zones, which was often, and he made us a fine defensive team. He was able to discourage passes into the post from the front and sides, steal passes and grab rebounds. Diagram 7-17 shows the basic slides in the 1–2–2 but player 1 can be used many different ways to alter these slides. In fact, the 1–2–2 is the most adjustable of all the defenses in the opinion of many coaches. The point man will put only *mild* pressure on the ball in his area usually. Some coaches have him really attack the ballhandler. However, most offensive teams put their weakest shooter on the point spot, one who is a good feeder. So unless a boy is hurting us with good outside shooting from the front, we try to prevent his passing into the high post area with our point man. So 1's responsibility is two-fold: prevent many baskets from the front spot, and stop passes to the high post. A good point man is able to keep himself between the ballhandler and the high post offensive player most of the time. He does this by constantly turning his head and by listening to his back-man teammate talk to him. (See Drills 1k and 3 in chapter 11.)

Diagram 7-16   Diagram 7-17

The point man must get a hand in the pass lanes any time two players try to play keep away from him. Unless the defense knows how to match-up against a 2–1–2 offense, the point man can get worked over at times by rapid passing. (Diagram 7-18.) Player 1 must get in the lane to stop this passing back and forth. (See Drill 3 in chapter 11.) It may become necessary to allow 2 or 3 to stunt up to help the point prevent easy shots, particularly if the team does not know how to use the match-up zone. (See Chapter 9 on Matching Zone Defense.)

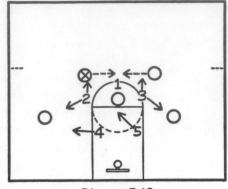

Diagram 7-18

Variations of Point Slides

1. As said earlier, even though Diagram 7-17 shows the basic moves of the point man, coaches many times alter the defense by adjusting this man. Some coaches use the *deep point drop* with this man. That is, when the ball is passed to the corner the point man slides as far as the deep post area. (Diagram 7-19.) It takes quite an athlete to do this, but if player 3 overplays the lane from the corner back to the wing, the point man can make this slide and still get back out front if the ball comes back there.

2. Other coaches use their point man to chase the ball all over the area in front of the foul line extended. The point man chases the ball and the wing men cover the area above the free throw lane and the wing. While this may not be the best use of a point man, many teams have gotten a lot of mileage out of a quick, hustling small player this way. He can play the pass lanes somewhat to help slow down the passes and to deflect or steal a few.

Diagram 7-20 shows the wing positions in the basic 1–2–2 when the ball is where the arrows point; of course 3's moves would be the same on the other side of the floor. The wing man turns his body toward the ball when it is out front, putting one hand toward the post, the other toward the man in his wing area. The wing man must pressure the ball hard in his area because most teams put their best shooters there. The wing must be on his man by the time the ball arrives if he is to hinder his shot. As the ball goes to the corner on his side he must stay close to the wing man. He will open toward the ball again and point one hand at the post, the other at the man in his area.

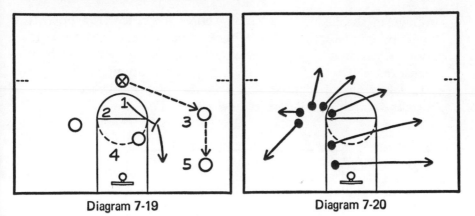

Diagram 7-19   Diagram 7-20

A good variation here is to put in a lane move by occasionally allowing the wing man to cover the pass lane back to the wing from the corner. This helps prevent the wing man from getting the ball in the scoring area and it also slows down the offensive passing game. (See Drill 4 in chapter 11.)

Another variation is to allow a trap with the back man when the ball is thrown into the corner. Neither of these moves is a containing move, of course, but allows a little variation and is good if not over-used. If it proves best to use these tactics more often, then the basic containing defense should be abandoned for the moment in favor of the more aggressive laning style. (See Drill 5 in chapter 11.)

When the ball is *two passes away*, the wing man will move to pressure the weak side goal area. Therefore, a tall man can be very effective on the wing spot. He can rebound well from this position and the extra height may cause the wing shooter some problems. Furthermore the wings do not have to be quite as quick or as good on defense as do the point and back men.

The Back Men

Along with the point men, the back men must be good athletes. It takes talk, hustle, and a lot of head-turning to play good back-line defense. Diagram 7-21 shows the basic positions of the back men when the ball is where the arrows point.

The slides of players 4 and 5 are basically lateral but they are not *flat*. (Diagram 7-22.) Proper sliding gives better defensive coverage in the high post area, as well as the crucial low post. It should be emphasized that the back men be cautioned never to play *too low,* too close to the goal. To play too low makes the defense have to cover more area and allows too much room for cutting in front of them by the offensive players. Diagram 7-23 shows the correct and incorrect positions.

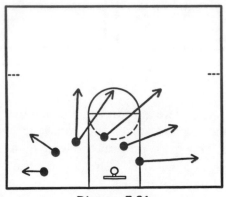

Diagram 7-21

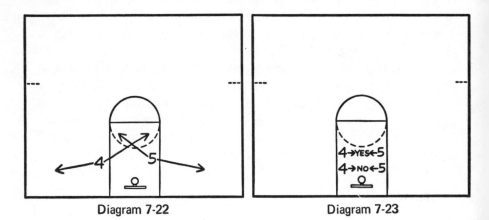

Diagram 7-22　　　　　　　　　　Diagram 7-23

The back men must both be expert at playing fundamental post defense. They must front in the low post, front cutters, keep the ball away from the post if at all possible, cover the corner hard, and rebound well.

The tandem rule can be used when necessary to cover the rovers on the 1–3–1 and 2–1–2 overload offenses. That is, when there are offensive men in both the high and low post, one of the defenders can start in the high post. The other can play the low post defense and rove the baseline until the ball is thrown to one corner. In recovering, the normal slides would be resumed. But any time the team stopped and set up again, the defenders could get back into regular position. (Diagram 7-24.) While it is usually best to have one certain man try to cover the high post and the other the low post in this situation, it is necessary for either to be able to go high or low. For example applying the tandem rule to the 1−2−2 offense which flashes its men into the high post area, either back man must stay with his man if he cuts into the high post.

As one can imagine there are many times that 4 and 5 can help avoid giving open shots by talking to each other. If one wants to continue on across the low post to the corner with a roving player, he can tell the other player and they can apply the tandem rule. Particularly when one man is forced to stay in the high post, it is better to allow the other back man to cross under or rove to the other corner than to make the regular slide. But if the point man is doing a good job of keeping the ball out of the high post, this measure will have to be used less frequently. (See Drill 9h in chapter 11.)

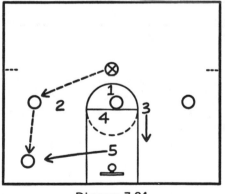

Diagram 7-24

The 1−3−1 Containing Zone

The 1−3−1 zone was devised to present a strong defensive attack in the high and low post areas and on the wings. At one time nearly every coach was attacking zones with a 1−3−1 standing offense and the 1−3−1 defense was custom-made to stop that. This defense has had much to do with the development of zone offenses over the past fifteen years. Coaches had to change offenses or get beaten.

In the containing positions as shown in Diagram 7-25 the point man, 1, plays on top of the circle, the wings are not spread too wide, only about two steps from the foul lane. The high post man, 3, will play behind the high offensive post while 5 will try to front anyone in the low post area and cover the first corner the ball goes to. The slides at the point, wings, and post are so similar to the 1−2−2 that repetition here is not needed. As one can see, the 1−3−1 is actually a 1−2−2 with the back men in high-low tandem positions.

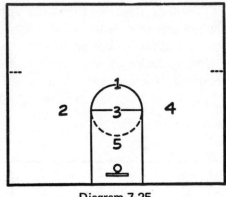

Diagram 7-25

The containing zones are effective to stop a team with a good inside attack or a strong rebounding game. By pressuring the high post from the front it allows the back men to exert maximum pressure on the vital inside area. Teams that can counter with a nice peripheral passing and outside shooting game will force the containing defensive team to adjust, of course, but this style of defense is calculated to negate the inside game, forcing the opponent to use its second best attack. It is appropriate, furthermore, for a defensive team with slow forwards or with a small team who wants to gang up on the defensive rebound. The containing style is most effective when used in combination with the laning style described next.

8

Coaching the
Laning Zone Defenses

The lane defenses vary from the containing ones in that the defenders push out into the pass lanes on players one pass from the ball in an attempt to break up the offensive passing and pattern game. The containing zones intend to shut off shots and passes in the top percentage scoring area. The lane zones are more aggressive and risky; they play the ball and hope to steal passes and force the offense out on the floor. The containing style is much more conservative in order to stop inside play, playing the man with the ball hard while trying to keep two or three players ready to stop the ballhandler's direct path to the goal. To contain is to allow peripheral passing. The lane zone expects to break up the pattern, the passing, and confuse the offense.

The lane zones require more adjusting and team speed. The front players need quick hands and the desire to play defense. The post man has to be a good defender because he must shut off the post area since he gets little help from the front. Easy post passes will ruin the lane defenses. The back men have to be ready to help recover for teammates that allow the offense to beat them. The lane defense is risky, so recoveries must be effective. All in all it takes a better team to play the lane defenses, a quicker and more adjustable team. And although the defensive risks are great, the possibilities of upsetting the opponent and stealing passes are considerable too.

THE 2–1–2 LANE ZONE

The 2–1–2 is a popular lane zone alignment. It allows for

good lane pressure out front and good high post coverage. Covering the low post is the toughest task. Diagram 8-1 shows the starting positions. The individuals except for the post man must use the open stance in lane-zone playing. More passes can be stolen in the open stance. The defense is playing the ball in the lane zone. In man-to-man pressing or laning the *man* is still the first concern but not in the lane zone.

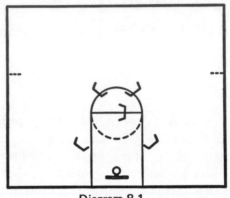

Diagram 8-1

Responsibilities of the Positions

The front men will cover the pass lanes from the front area to the wings when the ball is out front. If the ball goes to the wing, the nearest front man will cover the ballhandler while the other plays the pass back out front. With the ball in the corner the nearest wing man will pressure the lane back to the wing. (Diagram 8-2.) The back men cover the pass lane from the front to the low post when the ball is out front. As the ball goes to the wing the nearest back man will move to cover the wing until a front man can cover it. With the ball on the wing, the back man on the ball side will then cover the pass lane to the corner and baseline area. The opposite side back man will cover the low post. (Diagram 8-3.) Thus, the back men must cover the *low post area first* of all. Their second concern will be the wing and corner area of the ball side. If they forget their goal responsibilities, the defense will fail miserably because the post man is playing high. The post man must really work to keep the ball out of the high post. This is the second most crucial aspect to the defense. He does not have to worry about the low post, however, so he can work hard in his area to accomplish his all-important task.

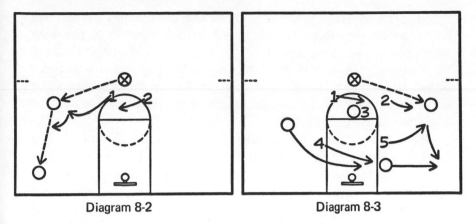

Diagram 8-2   Diagram 8-3

Defending the 1–3–1 Offense

Diagrams 8-4 and 8-5 show slides in covering the 1–3–1. The biggest thing to prevent is the point man splitting the two front defenders. Therefore, one front man takes the ball and the other plays a lane to the side. The front men must force the ball from the front spot to a wing before much pressure can be asserted. Using the hands is of prime importance in laning. Both guards should have their hands up and must concentrate on the ball, yet they have to watch to adjust as the possible receivers move so they can stay in or near the pass lane. They must keep the offense from beating them inside with a reverse or backdoor cut. They want to keep pushing the offense *out* in order to get open.

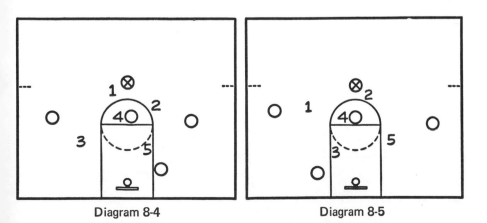

Diagram 8-4   Diagram 8-5

Diagrams 8-6 through 8-9 show the team slides as the ball moves around the floor. In Diagram 8-6 the ball moves to the wing while the roving base man pulls to the corner. Players 1 and 2 move toward the wing with 2 getting on the pass lane back to the point. Back man 5 covers the goal. In Diagram 8-7 3 covers the corner man with the ball while 1 gets in the pass lane back to the wing, forcing a high lob. The ball is moved to the opposite wing in Diagram 8-8 but notice how player 2 plays the point man. He had his lane coming from the wing and then jumped over to pressure the continuing reverse pass. The pass was made successfully anyway so 5 covers toward the *outside* momentarily until 2 can get to the wing. Player 3 moves to cover the low post while 4 continues to shut off the free throw area. In Diagram 8-9 player 5 has dropped off of the wing as 2 got to him in order to apply pressure to any inside pass. 3 covered the base cutter until 5 could help and quickly looked to prevent any other lay-in threat.

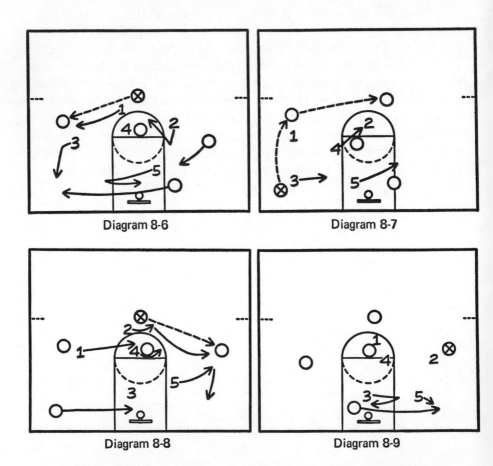

Diagram 8-6   Diagram 8-7

Diagram 8-8   Diagram 8-9

Defending the 2—1—2 Offense

A two-front offense, such as a 2—1—2 will cause the guards to split around the ballhandler and then make the same slides as against the 1—3—1. Diagrams 8-10 through 8-13 show slides against the 2—1—2. In Diagram 8-10 front man 1 pressures the outside of the ballhandler while 2 gets the lane to the other guard. Back man 3 would lane the forward up to foul line extended but must prevent him from getting the ball under the goal. Also, 5 will move far across the lane to prevent his back man from getting a pass in that area. With the ball on the wing 1 moves to cover the ball while 3 drops to cover the inside lane and 2 pressures the top of the circle. In Diagrams 8-11 through 8-13 the defenders move to cover against the 1—3—1 offense. The main difference is in meeting the original lineup. Once the ball is in motion the slides are the same. Practicing to meet the different attacks will enable the defenders to become adept at handling them.

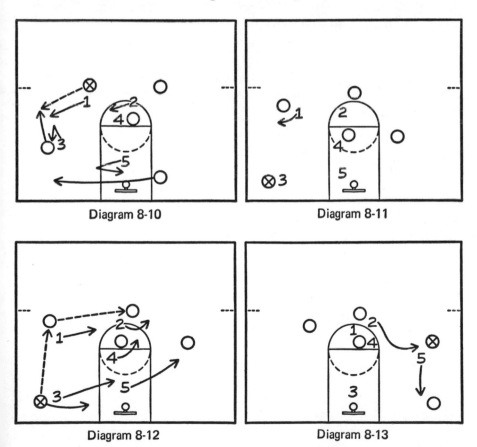

Diagram 8-10   Diagram 8-11

Diagram 8-12   Diagram 8-13

The 2–1–2 lane zone may be spread to the half-line and used as a press. Ideally the defense would try to trap at the half-line. Diagram 8-14 shows an outside lane trap at the half-line with a forward-to-guard move. Player 2 forces the ballhandler to the outside. 5 jumps to trap if he can get to the ball quickly. If no trap occurs the defense will play whatever half-court defense they are told to fall into in the scoring area, probably a 2–1–2 lane zone. If the trap is set but fails to get possession of the ball, the players must recover hard into the scoring area and re-set their defense. The slides in the press are just as described earlier for half-court traps (Chapter 3). The ball must be kept out of the post area on this press, it should be emphasized.

While a guard-to-guard trap could be set in the outside lane also, on the 2–1–2 most guard-to-guard traps will be set in the middle lane. The guard on the ballhandler will try to overplay the outside as a variation to force this trap. (Diagram 8-15.) The back men would float in the outside lanes while 4 zones the goal area as in all middle lane traps. (Chapter 3) Again, a hard recovery must be made if the trap is beaten.

Diagram 8-16 shows the guard-to-forward outside lane trap that can be used if the team wants to continue pressing on into the scoring area. The coach can use the 2–1–2 to press at the half-line only and then fall into a more containing style, or he can continue trapping and pressing with the 2–1–2 in the scoring area as well. (See Drills 2-6 in chapter 11 for lane zones.)

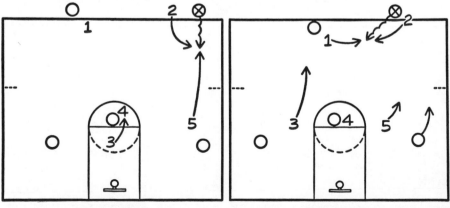

Diagram 8-14   Diagram 8-15

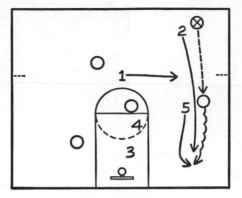

Diagram 8-16

THE 1–2–2 LANE ZONE

The 1–2–2 lane zone has the same characteristics as the 2–1–2 lane, only the slides are different. Diagram 8-17 shows the original positions with 4 and 5 ready to tandem. Diagrams 8-18 through 8-20 show the slides against a 1–3–1 offense. The back men may need to use the tandem and rover rules as referred to in chapter 6.

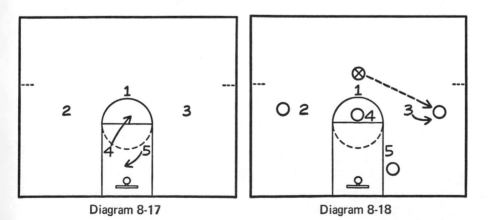

Diagram 8-17   Diagram 8-18

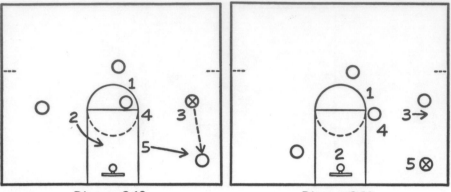

Diagram 8-19   Diagram 8-20

As one may observe the 1–2–2 is very adaptable to laning. The biggest problem is getting 4 and 5 to be able to tandem well enough to shut off the high post pass and the low post rover but it can be done, particularly if the point man helps pressure the post some, too.

In Diagram 8-18 wing man 3 tries to keep the wing man from getting the ball in scoring range by playing his lane. 2 does the same on the other side while 4 and 5 shut down the high and low post. The ball is at the wing in Diagram 8-19 so 2 moves to protect the goal. As the ball goes to the corner in the final diagram in the series, 3 gets into the lane back to the wing.

Many teams will attack the 1–2–2 with the 2–1–2 offense. Diagrams 8-21 through 8-23 show the slides against the 2–1–2 offense. In Diagram 8-21 player 1 takes the ball as he usually does. Player 3 on the open weak side will rise up somewhat but usually does not come any higher than the dotted line. The offense is already pretty far out on the floor and that is the aim of the defense.

The 2–1–2 can cause some problems to the defense but with good hustle and execution the defense can do a good job. In Diagram 8-22 notice the slides as the ball goes to the wing area. 5 will help 3 some but cannot leave the base-line area very far; he receives some help from 2. As the ball goes back around in Diagrams 8-23 and 8-24 the defense shifts to keep in 1–2–2 lane position. Players 4 and 5 may change positions to cover the left corner, or 5 can rove the base-line as shown. If the ball is kept out of the post, the defense can be very effective.

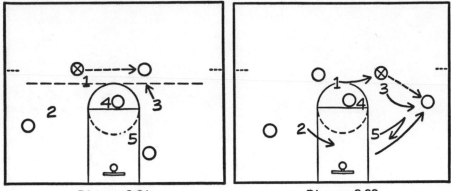

Diagram 8-21   Diagram 8-22

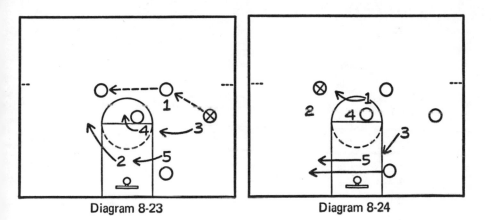

Diagram 8-23   Diagram 8-24

THE 1–3–1 LANE ZONE

The 1–3–1 lane zone has the same principles of the other lane zones and has similar slides to the 1–2–2. Diagram 8-25 shows the original positions and 8-26 through 8-28 show the slides against a 1–3–1 offense. The back men are in tandem positions to begin with, of course. The high post man plays in front of the offensive high post. The wing men, 2 and 3, try to front the wings and force them out on the floor.

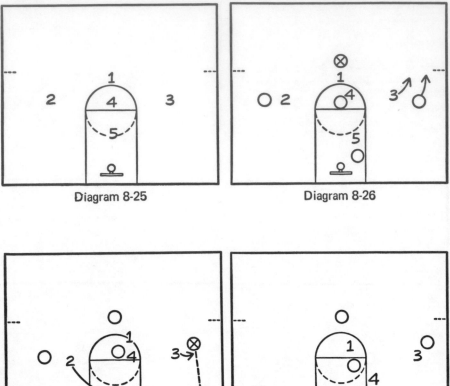

Diagram 8-25   Diagram 8-26

Diagram 8-27   Diagram 8-28

The wings must be sure to keep alert for the backdoor move by wing men in their area. The wing men must cover the deep post area when 5 has to pull to the corner as in Diagrams 8-27 and 8-28. Player 2 in those diagrams will move as far into the lane as he must but *must* get back out to cover his wing when the ball reverses as in the regular 1—3—1 and 1—2—2. This must be emphasized. Player 4 keeps the high post shut down by fronting. This is the basic difference from the 1—2—2. A quick review will show how similar the 1—3—1 and 1—2—2 slides are. Diagrams 8-29 through 8-34 show the slides against the 2—1—2 offense. In Diagram 8-29 player 1 takes the ball as he overplays the guard-to-guard pass lane. Player 3 would not go any higher than the dotted line roughly. He tries to help 1 when he can but must still cover the wing. Diagram 8-31 shows the ball in the corner with 5 covering the ball, 3 in the lane to the wing and 2 covering the goal.

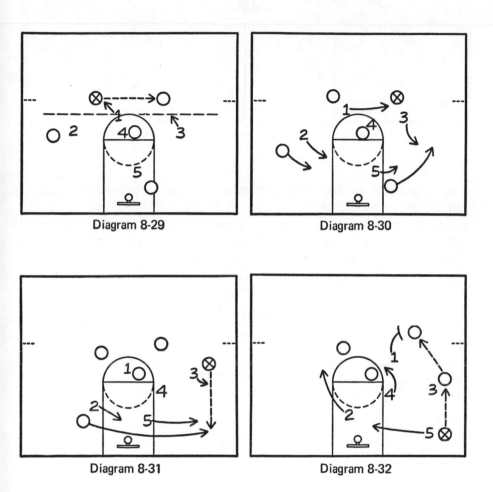

Diagram 8-29   Diagram 8-30

Diagram 8-31   Diagram 8-32

In Diagrams 8-33 and 8-34 the ball is swung around the top. Player 1 overplays the guard-to-guard lane again in Diagram 8-33 and player 2 would come about as high as the dotted line to help player 1. In Diagram 8-34 player 5 is in the corner again while 2 is in the lane out front and 3 covers the goal.

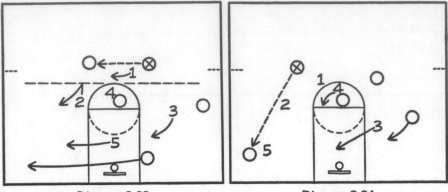

Diagram 8-33   Diagram 8-34

There is another effective way to help player 1 cover the front area. Instead of letting the wings help the point man against a two-guard front, the high post man may shift out. (Diagram 8-35.) This opens up the crucial high post so the wing man on the side that 4 moves up on, player 3 in Diagram 8-35, fills in at the high post. The move is risky but is a possible option. If the ball is passed into the open wing area, 3 will scramble out and 4 will get in the high post, although the two men could rotate positions instead.

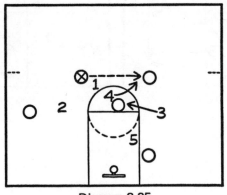

Diagram 8-35

The 1–2–2 and 1–3–1 lane zones are also adaptable to half-court or full-court pressing. The traps must be ruled just as in the 2–1–2. The laning zones make a tough defense for the right team. For other teams lacking overall speed but wanting to gain some of the benefits of the lane zones, they may use a basic containing zone but allow the lane from the corner to the side to be covered, or possibly allow the quards, or wings, to jump into lanes occasionally. As has been mentioned before, any time the front men lane the front area the high post man must play very aggressively to keep the ball out of the post.

As long as the coach is careful to drill to protect the high post and the basket, the lane zones can be very effective. Boys like to play this style because they can really move and stunt in it. Combined with the containing style a team can use the same formation and basic slides yet cause the offense fits by moving in and out from laning to containing. Since one style does not allow peripheral passing while the other does, the offense must adjust its game with each defensive change. It is not done easily.

9

Effecting the
Matching Zone Defense

The matching zone defense is one of the latest significant developments in defense. To assist in describing what is involved in the match-up defense, one could say it is an attempt to have a consistent one-on-one defensive situation with a zone defense. It is man-to-man to a point. That is, each defender has responsibility for one man within his general zone. Of course, it would not be any particular man—just whoever is there at any given moment. The defender would not follow this man all over the front court as he would if he were playing a man-to-man defense. The match-up thus allows for a lot of one-on-one coverage to try to counter against the overload zone attacks. Years ago coaches could expect pretty good results each time they faced zones by trying to overload their offense so that some defensive man was forced to cover two men in his area. The match-up is calculated to negate the effects of the overload by matching the offensive setup one for one.

Because of the success of the match-up, coaches have been forced to get to work to develop new offensive counters which use more player movement. Player movement, when done well, will cause the matching zones far more trouble than the old standard ball movement offenses which have little shifting of personnel. The problem of *staying* matched up against a cutting offense has become basic for the defense now.

Although the matching zones are harder to teach and more practice time-consuming, many coaches have found them to be great neutralizers. Particularly when the defensive coach has a good scouting report on the opponent's zone offense, he can hope to upset a stronger team. If the defense can adjust to the offense quickly, the opponent may find it difficult to get many first shots closer than twenty feet, provided the difference in talent is not too great.

This chapter will describe the basics of matching up such as rotating, slides, and the rules necessary to help the defense *stay* matched up with the offense. The following chapter will show the specific moves when matching up with the 2–3, 1–2–2 and 1–3–1.

DEFENDING THE MATCHED OFFENSIVE LINE-UP

There are two types of fronts the defense may use in the matching defense, the two-front and the one-front. The two-front (2–1–2) would already be matched up out front with any two-front zone offense. It is easy for the rest of the defense to match the initial offensive formation in this case. Diagram 9-1 shows the way matching is done when the defense has hustled back and is ready for the offense. The front man nearest the ball would take the ballhandler. In the diagram player 1 takes the ball and the rest of the matching is simple. Player 2 takes the first man to the right of 1; 3 takes the first man to the left of 1; 5 takes anyone in the post; and 4 takes the first player to the right of 2. When a player cannot see anyone immediately to defend, he will drop into the free throw lane area and help out.

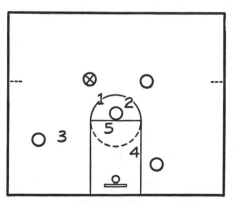

Diagram 9-1

If the team uses a one-front (1−2−2 or 1−3−1) as their starting defensive formation, they will readily match with any one-front offense. (Diagram 9-2.) Player 1 would take the offensive point man. Player 2 would take the first player to 1's left while 3 would take the first player to 1's right. Post men 4 and 5 must take the men in the high and low post and cover the corners when necessary. They work as a team: if one is in the high post, the other is in low and if one is in the corner, the other protects the basket.

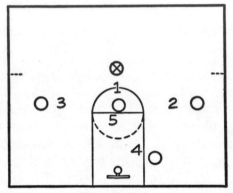

Diagram 9-2

DEFENDING THE MISMATCHED OFFENSIVE LINE-UP

The problem of matching the initial offensive formation is more difficult when the fronts do not match up. To get into a matched position the defense must *rotate*. There are three ways a team may rotate—right, left, and double. To illustrate, a two-front defense is mismatched against a 1−3−1 offense. Diagram 9-3 shows a rotation to the right to get matched, while Diagram 9-4 shows a rotation left. In Diagram 9-3 player 1 takes the ball and the outside defenders rotate to the right with him. The same idea is followed as before in that 2 then has the first man to 1's left, 3 has the first man to 1's right, and 4 has the first man to 2's right. Player 5 defends the post. Diagram 9-4 shows 2 taking the ballhandler and the defense rotating left with the same principles.

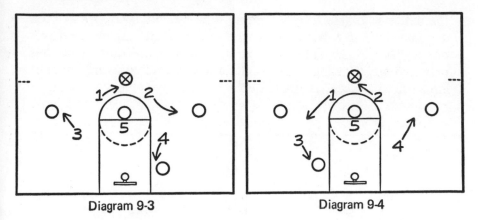

Diagram 9-3   Diagram 9-4

Some teams will use only a single rotation such as that described. When a team can rotate both ways as the situation demands it, they are able to *double rotate.* Naturally, it takes a better team to be able to do so, to rotate freely in either direction. It is best to be able to do this, however, so that the defense can rotate toward the overloaded area of the offense. As in Diagrams 9-3 and 9-4 the rotations went in the direction of the largest number of offensive players.

It is worthwhile to match up even if a team cannot double rotate. When we had small guards and a 6' 1" forward we still could use the match-up but we did not double rotate. We would single rotate to the right awhile and move him over to the left back side. Then we would move him to the right back spot and rotate left. By doing this we always rotated the small forward up instead of down toward the baseline and goal area where his size would hurt us. We did this from the 2—1—2 formation.

A one-front defense would have to rotate to match-up with any two-front offense. Diagrams 9-5 and 9-6 show right and left rotations to meet the 2—1—2 offensive line-up. Player 1 keys the rotation either way and the players follow his lead. Players take men to the right and left of player 1 as has been indicated before.

The one-front defense is a good one for the team with a small point man because he always gets to play out front. It is best that the team also have two good back defenders for the 4 and 5 post spots. If they have only one good inside defender, the 2—1—2 will usually be better.

A key worth emphasizing is that the man who takes the ballhandler should do so very obviously in order that the rest of the defense be able to adjust more quickly and easily. We like for our man to step toward the offensive man a step or two and yell out that he has the ball. Everyone then must adjust quickly for the best defense. Getting back on defense fast and adjusting quickly are basic to a successful match-up.

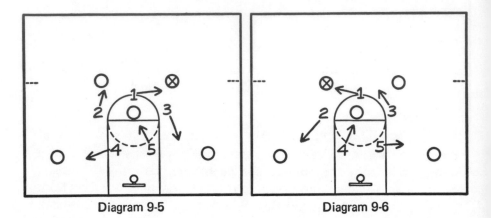

Diagram 9-5   Diagram 9-6

MATCHING UP FROM THE FAST BREAK

Once the team understands the methods of getting matched up originally they will want to try to use the match-up in a scrimmage type of situation. But first they must drill on getting matched up around the ball when the ball has beaten some of the defenders into the front court. If a defender has stopped the ball in an area other than his own, the defense will just have to fill up the remaining positions in the order shown in Diagram 9-7.

Diagram 9-8 shows all five players being able to recover into their own original 2–3 spots. In the case when the ball beats some of the defenders back, it is to be understood that the players will not be able to go to their original spots and then rotate to the ball. This would give up easy points. First they must *protect the goal*, then *stop the ball*. Everyone fills in around the ball after this. This is called "stopping the ball and matching up around it." It is a must for the fast break defense.

Diagram 9-7 illustrates the goal and ball coverage. The next areas to cover are the ones adjacent to the ballhandler. The foul area must also be stopped. Diagram 9-9 shows another possibility on sequence of coverage, this time with the ball being stopped out front.

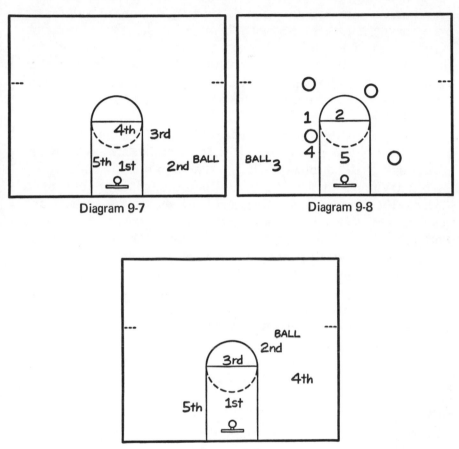

Diagram 9-7

Diagram 9-8

Diagram 9-9

Thus, the idea is to cover the goal, stop the ball and then defend the men in the spots nearest the ballhandler. The forwards will try to fall to the first of the underneath spots they get to and the guards will try to end up at either front spot. If this does not quite work out, the players can adjust to their desired spot at an opportune time similar to the manner of exchanging to get one's own assignment in the man-to-man defense. Much of this will come naturally to players; and drilling it on a full-court basis will firmly establish the habits of matching up around the ball when recovering from the fast break.

SLIDES TO BE LEARNED AT EACH POSITION

Coaches who seldom deal with zone defense may not realize how confusing it can be for boys to have to learn different zone positions. Some coaches have become soured on zones because they have had little success with them. Often the reason for failure is poor teaching. The coach must acquaint each player with the movements to be made at his position. He must also realize that not many of his boys will be able to play more than one position. There are some athletes who will be able to learn to play all spots well. But generally most boys will be able to play no more than two positions. (See Drill 8 in chapter 11.)

The front men must learn the three basic slides as shown in Diagrams 9-10 through 9-12. The dots represent the general position the player should assume when the ball is at the spot to which the arrows point. Diagram 9-10 shows the verticle and lateral movements the guard must make to cover any two-out offense. We can call this an "oblique" slide. Diagrams 9-11 and 9-12 show how differently the guard will move against the one-front offenses. In Diagram 9-11 the left guard has rotated to the point, a right rotation. He will have a verticle slide in this case. We call this an "I" slide to describe his up-down move. In Diagram 9-12 the other guard rotates to the point, a left rotation, and this puts the left guard at the wing spot. In this position he must operate like a forward or wing man. His slide is a right angular one, an "L" slide. Therefore, a front man will have to know three basic slides to play the match-up. Since it is more complicated to play than a person might think at first, it is important to explain these slides precisely to the players. It tends to give them more awareness about their position.

Diagrams 9-13 through 9-15 illustrate the back men's slides. Against the two-front offenses the back men have an easy lateral slide. (Diagram 9-13.) They cover anyone in their area from the wing to the corner and fall back into the goal area with the ball on the opposite side. Diagram 9-14 shows the post slides when the defense is in 1—2—2 alignment. The post man must learn to work the corner to post slide and how to defend the low post area. In Diagram 9-15 the two-front defense has rotated right, making the left back man go to the wing spot where he has the regular "L" slide.

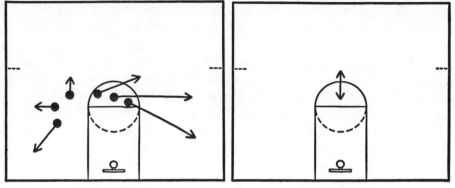

Diagram 9-10   Diagram 9-11

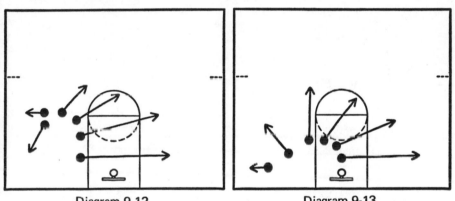

Diagram 9-12   Diagram 9-13

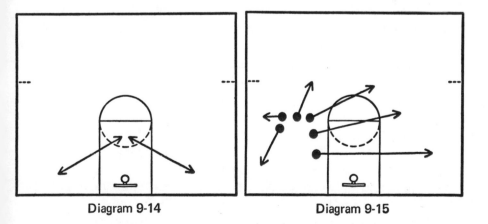

Diagram 9-14   Diagram 9-15

The post slides will also have to be learned by the back men, especially if a team tries to match up with the 1−2−2. When a team matches up with the 2−3 they can keep one man in the middle almost constantly and his slides would be the simple but demanding slides shown in Diagram 9-16. In addition the back men should be drilled to be baseline rovers when it becomes necessary to apply that rule, as when matching up some 1−3−1 offenses or whenever an offensive post man stays quite high as the ball is reversed. (Diagram 9-17.)

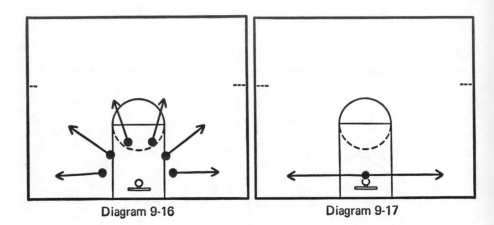

Diagram 9-16   Diagram 9-17

The post man plays very tough in the keyhole area. He will try to keep the ball out of the middle, especially in the low post area. How to play at the foul line area will depend on two things: the ability of the middle man to intimidate anyone from shooting who gets the ball there, and whether the guards are helping keep the ball out of the middle or not. If the coach decides his post man can afford to play behind the offensive high post, then that defender has an easier job. This does not necessarily make for the best defense, but it tends to keep the middle man out of foul trouble and in good rebounding position. If the guards will help by playing a containing style, the ball can be kept out of the vital middle area to a satisfactory level. If the coach decides to have his post man play aggressively at the high post, the man can try to keep his hand between the ball and the offensive post man, but he cannot afford to front the high post area like he must in the low post. To do so would put too much pressure on the back men to defend the goal area. The men who play in the post are really the key defensive men. They must dominate this area. It has to be a real challenge to them and they must accept it for the defense to go.

SPECIFIC MATCH-UP RULES

It is essential that the matching zone team employ the general zone rules that are listed in chapter 6 first of all. The following are rules which are basic to the match-up, while the listing in chapter 6 applies to all zone styles, including the match-up.

1. *One man in your area*—if he has the ball, pressure him hard in a good wide stance. If he is one pass away, drop off a little into the middle unless he is an exceptional shooter. If he is two passes from the ball, drop as far into the middle of the defense as possible and still be able to get to him when the ball does.

2. *Two men in your area*—if possible, guard the man farthest from the goal. You should receive some help from your teammates on the other man. Naturally, if the ball is two passes away, drop into the middle of the defense but anticipate reaching the far one if the ball reverses back around.

3. *No one in your area*—drop into the free throw area, the middle of the defense. Plug up the middle and wait for someone to move into your area.

4. *Deep cut to the corner on the ball side*—the outside defender drops as player 1 does in Diagram 9-18. This is like the regular cutter rule. The post man must pick him up and go to the corner with him. The other back man, 5, and the weak side front or wing, 2, must cover the post and goal area. (See Drill 9c in chapter 11.)

5. *Shallow, or wide cut to the corner on the ball side*—the outside defender, 1, goes with his man toward the adjacent zone area and releases the next zone defender, 3, to slide down and cover the cutter. (Diagram 9-19.) This cut is not quite the threat the deep cut is and may be handled this way without involving as much shifting of personnel. (See Drill 9b in chapter 11.)

6. *Dribble-pulling on the perimeter*—when a dribbler pulls a defender out of position, the defender stays with the ball and the outside defenders rotate with him. Diagrams 9-20 and 9-21 show two dribble pulls. In the first of the diagrams player 1 goes with the ballhandler while 2 and 5 rotate his direction. In the second diagram 2 goes with the ball and players 1 and 3 rotate his way. (See Drill 9d in chapter 11.)

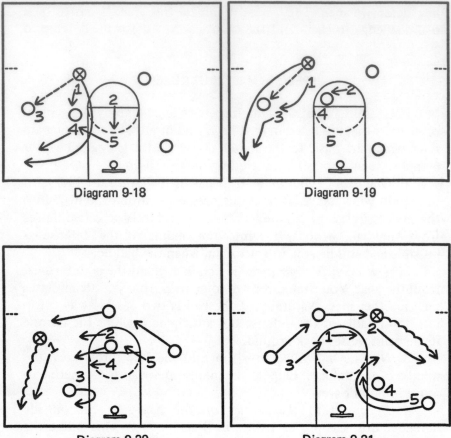

Diagram 9-18   Diagram 9-19

Diagram 9-20   Diagram 9-21

Against teams who do this a lot, the ball defender can overplay the dribbler and often stop his move. Or he may go only into the edge of the next defensive area and be released off the man by the next defender. The coach must choose which method he prefers.

In drilling the match-up it is important to set up the different rule situations and go over them at half-court and then try them full court. To be most effective the team must drill against all the known offensive moves of the opponent prior to the game. Once the defense is familiar with the opponent's man-to-man offense and its two or three zone moves, it can adjust to bother the opponent considerably. The beautiful thing about the match-up is that there are only a limited number of offensive moves. When the rules are learned well, a rule application should cover any move the team faces. If the coach is at a loss as to how to cover a specific move and cannot improvise a stopgap, he will have to go to a different defense that night. As one gains experience with the match-up, he will find fewer and fewer unfamiliar moves. The defense gains the advantage as the year progresses. There are only certain moves the offense can use, so when the match-up players learn their rules well, they can cover almost anyone's moves if the difference in talent is not too great.

To facilitate learning these rules and the general zone rules we always compile the list on a sheet and give our players homework to study in addition to our explaining and drilling.

It has been helpful to us to divide both our man-to-man and zone team drills in half. On alternate days we go through half of the basic drills of each defense. For example on Monday we might use the following team drills:

Man-to-man	*Zone*
1. Recoveries (Drill 13 in chapter 5)	1. Cutter-to-goal rule (Drill 9a in chapter 11)
2. Traps (Drill 12d in chapter 5)	
3. Split the post (Drill 9f in chapter 5)	2. Wide-cut rule (Drill 9b in chapter 11)
	3. Deep-cut rule (Drill 9c in chapter 11)

On Tuesday we would drill perhaps the following:

Man-to-man	*Zone*
1. Switching (Drill 9b, d, e in chapter 5)	1. Ball into post rule (Drill 9i in chapter 11)
2. Shuffle defense (Drill 9c in chapter 5)	2. Screen rule (Drill 9e in chapter 11)
3. Stop the dribble and get into lanes (Drill 12e in chapter 5)	3. Rover rule (Drill 9h in chapter 11)

It takes only a few mintues each day to do this and by mid-season the team can stay sharp by reviewing each team drill once a week. Recovering and trapping are the same in either defense, incidentally. We believe that the team approach to drilling is superior to the individual drills. However, individual drills still have an important place since they help teach the skills that make up the team effort. As a team progresses through the season, we drop the individual drills gradually in favor of more team drills. If a boy has trouble with a specific part, we will work him on that individual aspect whenever we must.

If the coach will begin his early practices by grounding his team with fundamental man-to-man defensive play, it is a simple and logical step to move into the rules for zone defense described in chapter 6. Then, if the coach desires to go on deeper into zone play he can teach the specific match-up principles. The final step in utilizing the match-up is to select a formation from which to begin the defense. As one reads the discussion of the various formations in the following chapter, he should bear in mind a recommendation: go so far as to utilize the match-up only when you want your basic team defense to be zone; otherwise, too much practice time must be used if it is not a truly integral part of the defense.

10

Matching Up
with the Basic Zones

The coach may decide to match-up with any zone formation. In this chapter we will show how to match-up with the 2–3, 1–2–2, and 1–3–1. More important we will illustrate how to use the principles and rules mentioned in chapters 6 and 9 in order to stay matched up against some zone offense moves.

THE 2–3 MATCHING ZONE

Diagram 10-1 shows the starting positions from which the defense will adjust to match-up with the offense. It is tremendously important for the defenders to try to get back as often as possible into these starting positions before the offense can get into the front court. The players will always try to go to these original areas and adjust anew each time the offense moves the ball into the front court. There will be many times that the offense will beat the defense down the floor, however. When the ball gets into play in the front court before all five defenders are set and ready, the defense must match-up around the ball as best they can by using their knowledge of the match-up rules in chapter 9.

Personnel placement will follow conventional lines with the guards playing the front positions, forwards the back ones, and the big man in the middle. This defense can be used by big or small teams.

Attacking the Two-Front Zone Offenses

Since the defense is a two-front defense the problem of matching with the two-front offenses (2–1–2, 2–2–1, 2–out overload) is a small one. The front men are already matched. (Diagram 10-2.) So, one of the guards flexes toward the ball as it nears the scoring area. He must meet the ballhandler with pressure at the scoring area fringe. The other front defender opens toward the ball and is ready to cover the other guard if the ball goes to him; he tries more to hinder any passing attempts into the high post.

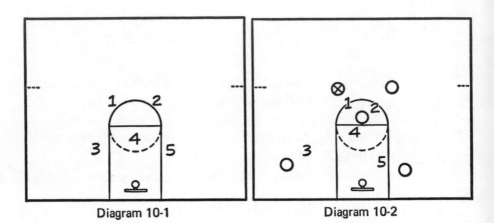

Diagram 10-1   Diagram 10-2

Player 1 has the ballhandler while player 2 has the first man to 1's right, the other guard. The following list of *coverage plans* will explain how the rest of the players all match-up as the ball comes into play.

Player 1—He either takes the ballhandler or else the first man to the *left* of 2 when 2 takes the ballhandler.

Player 2—The same assignment as 1. He takes the ballhandler or the first player to 1's *right* when 1 takes the ball.

Player 3—He takes the first player to the *left* of 1.

Player 4—He guards the middle. If there is no one in the middle, check the *tandem rule* in chapter 6; he will probably have to cover the corner.

Player 5—He takes the first player to the *right* of 2.

Diagrams 10-3 and 10-4 show how the 2–3 would adjust to match-up with some two-front offenses. If one will go over the list of coverage plans as he checks each diagram, he will see how simply the initial matching is done.

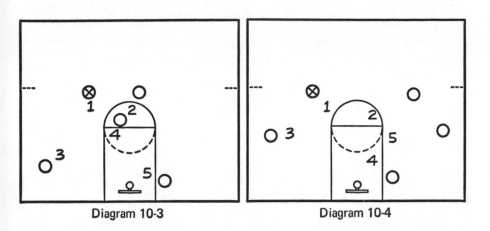

Diagram 10-3   Diagram 10-4

Attacking the One-Front Zone Offenses

Because the 2–3 is a two-front defense, the one-front offenses present more of a problem in matching. More teams will try a one-front offense against this defense, as one would expect. In order to match to a one-front offense (1–2–1 or 1–3–1) the defense has to rotate. They may rotate right or clockwise only, left or counterclockwise only, or they may use both.

In Diagram 10-5 the defense has rotated right to match a 1–3–1 offense. Player 1 calls out early that he will take the ball and flexes out to put pressure on the ballhandler. All defensive players *adjust to the player who takes the ballhandler,* in this case player 1. In Diagram 10-6 player 2 takes the ballhandler and the defense rotates left. Remember that the defense tries to start in the same 2–3 spots, then match-up. They want to *show* the 2–3 to the other team first, then *rotate to match* them.

Diagrams 10-7 and 10-8 show rotations right and left to match the 1–2–2 but the tandem rule for the high and low post coverage must be applied to make this move work.

When it is necessary to try to hide a short forward or a poor back line defender, a team will use one rotation at a time. This is the defense in which we had a 6' 1" forward so we would rotate one way for awhile, then move him to the other side and rotate the other way awhile, and so on through the game. Diagrams 10-9 and 10-10 show how this was done; the small forward is marked "S." One can see that the small player is *rotated away from* which puts him on the wing in each case. To have him under the goal in low post defensive position was what we hoped to avoid.

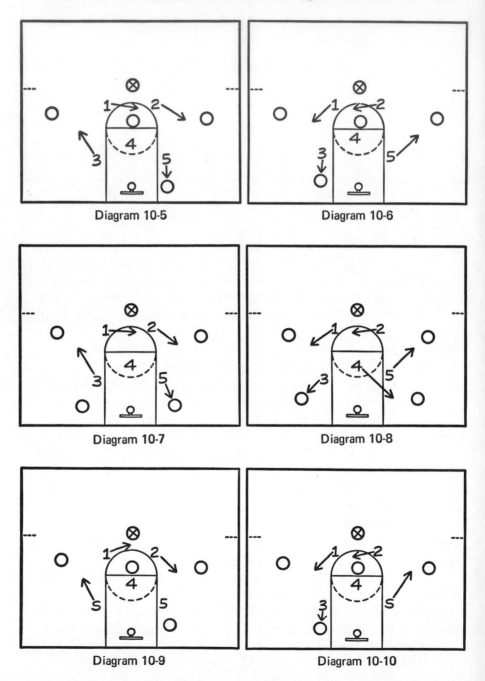

Diagram 10-5   Diagram 10-6

Diagram 10-7   Diagram 10-8

Diagram 10-9   Diagram 10-10

By analyzing all the 2–3 match-up slides the alert coach can understand why we chose to match up from this formation when we had two 5' 10" guards, 6' 1" and 6' 2" forwards and a fine defensive middle man. We could use our two quick guards to ball-hawk and they were pulled under the goal infrequently enough. We could keep our good shot-blocker in the middle nearly all the time. The only place we got hurt was on the rover rule; we were at a disadvantage whenever one of our forwards had to rove the base.

Using the Rules to Stay Matched

We will diagram a few offensive moves that teams have used against our zones to show how a team would use the rules to maintain the match-up. In Diagram 10-11 the defense rotated left to match the original 1–3–1 offensive alignment. After the wing man passed to the corner he cut through to the goal. Player 1 applied the cutter to the goal rule and went two or three steps, called out that the cutter was going through and then moved out ready to cover any new man who would move into his area. Players 4 and 5 absorbed the cutter while 2 jammed into the middle of the defense since no one was left in his area momentarily. Player 1 will defend the first offensive man to the right of the ball, the point man, as he moves to receive the ball from the corner man.

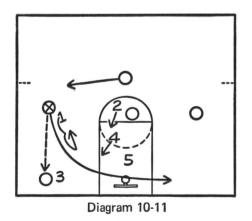

Diagram 10-11

Diagram 10-12 shows a cross pattern from a 2–3 alignment.

It may be covered either of two ways. The defense begins matched against this two-front attack. As the guard passes to the wing player, 1 applies the cutter to the goal rule and calls out "cutter." Player 2's man cuts the ball-side corner. This cut amounts to a deep corner cut and can be covered with that rule. That is, 1 would cover in the high post area, 4 would cover the corner, and 5 would move up to cover the post for 4. Player 2 would cover the deep post weak side for 5. A second way to cover this would be for 5 to apply the rover rule if he feels 4 cannot cover the corner. Player 2 would rotate back to take 5's place either way. The coach must decide which rule to have his team apply. After that it is simple enough to cover.

It might be well to carry out this offensive maneuver to include the reversal of the ball. Diagram 10-13 shows the ball reversed with the wing cutting to the second corner. Player 3 covers the first pass and drops in as this man cuts to the opposite corner. Player 1 meets the new point man and 2 moves up to the wing on the right side. The second corner can be covered by whichever back man (4 or 5) remained in the post when they cover the first corner. However, if the offensive man in the post stays very high, it may be necessary to apply the rover rule once again and have the same player who covered the first corner, 4, to *rove* and cover the second one as well. This is a matter accomplished best by the two men talking. Regardless, the moves can be covered quite well with the match-up.

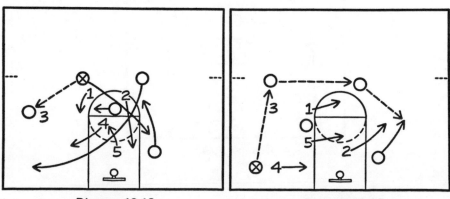

Diagram 10-12   Diagram 10-13

MATCHING UP WITH THE 1–2–2

Diagram 10-14 shows the original 1–2–2 set-up. The best tall defenders will play on the back line, the toughest spots to play in the 1–2–2.

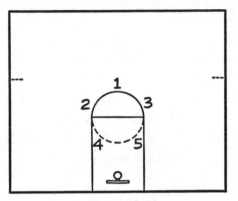

Diagram 10-14

The point man should be a good defender and since he will key the rotations, it is best if he is a smart player. The weaker defenders may be put on the wing spots. Diagrams 10-15 and 10-16 show the match-up against the 1–2–2 and 1–3–1 offenses. The tandem rule may be applied to match with the post man if the defense is not successful in covering the post and corners the regular way. Therefore, in Diagram 10-16, 4 has gone into the high post while 5 defends the low area. They should be able to interchange in order to be most effective.

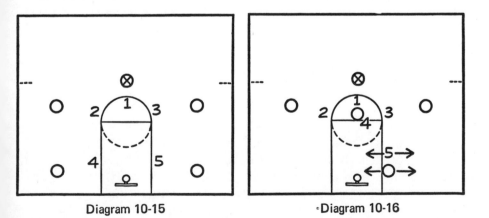

Diagram 10-15   •Diagram 10-16

As one can see it is easy to match-up against the one-front offenses. To apply the same coverage plans as we did in the 2–3, the 1–2–2 players will cover the following men in the match-up:

Player 1 takes the ballhandler and puts good pressure on him. Do not have him pressure too hard out front if the point offensive player is a poor shooter so that he can jam the middle more. If his man does not have the ball, he fills in the free throw circle area to help stop the middle.

Player 2 takes the first player to the *left* of 1.

Player 3 takes the first player to the right of 1.

Player 4 takes the first player to the left of 2.

Exception: When using the tandem rule he guards either the high or low post, opposite of player 5.

Player 5 takes the first player to the right of 3.

Exception: The tandem rule as with player 4.

Note: Players 4 and 5 will learn that when the defense rotates to match a two-front offense one of these players will be rotated into the middle to play post defense and the other will become a regular back man. The above principles still apply.

Rotating to Match the Two-Front Offenses

Player 1 will key the rotation by taking one of the opponent's guards. If the defense can rotate both ways, right and left, he will take the ballhandler normally. If only the single direction rotation is used, he must always take the guard on the side to which the defense wants to rotate. Diagram 10-17 shows a rotation left; Diagram 10-18 has a right rotation and Diagram 10-19 illustrates how the point man would take the guard without the ball in an instance in which his team can rotate only one way—left in this case. All diagrams show a 2–1–2 offense.

Rotating to Match the 2–2–1 Offense

The 2–2–1 is occasionally used against the 1–2–2 and if well-executed can cause some problems. Diagrams 10-20 and 10-21 show the right and left rotations to cover the 2–2–1 formation. The back men will have to practice to be able to cover the baseline man and flash cuts into the high post. By talking, the shifts can be made well enough. If the team fails to cover correctly, the one baseline player will have to rove with the offensive baseline man.

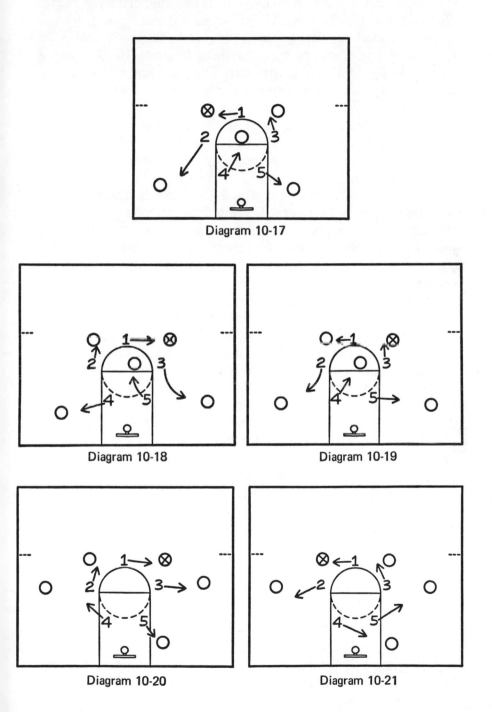

Diagram 10-17

Diagram 10-18

Diagram 10-19

Diagram 10-20

Diagram 10-21

Using the Rules to Stay Matched Up

After the original match-up is made the offensive moves discussed for the 2–3 would be covered the same way by the 1–2–2. Therefore, let us look at some different moves to illustrate further how to stay matched. Diagram 10-22 shows a normal 1–3–1 ball-side corner cut. The deep cut rule would be applied as 4 pulls to the corner and player 5 and 3 adjust. A wide cut to the ball-side corner is made in Diagram 10-23. Player 1 has 2 slide off to the corner to cover this move. Player 3 moves up to cover the first man to the right of 1 as he must. Player 1 can alert his teammates to the proper move by calling out either, "deep cut" or "wide cut."

Diagram 10-24 shows a typical 2–1–2 screen attack. Player 5 is squeezed in on the screen. He now has two men in his area as the ball moves one pass away. He must try to take the farther one from the goal. He moves up two steps and takes one step toward the outside to be able to cover the post man who pulls to the corner.

The 1–4 attack is a common one against zones. We have found that most ball-side corner cuts can be handled with the deep cut rule against this alignment except for the cut the point man might make swinging out wide past the wing to the corner and the opposite wing's cut as shown in the diagram here. In Diagram 10-25 any offensive man except the wing ballhandler could feasibly cut to the ball-side corner. If the point man cuts through deep, it is best for 4 to cover him. If the post man 4 is guarding cuts there, it is certainly easy for him to go with him. These are deep-cut rule applications. If the man 5 is lined up with goes to the ball corner, it is easy for 5 to tell 4 to stay and that he will use the rover rule and cover the corner. He *may* be covered by 4, 5, or 3. The coach will want to decide which adjustment would be best. This is where scouting comes in handy. It is best treated as a rover option by letting 5 or possibly 3 cover. If the deep cut rule is applied, 4 would cover but this is not best in this case.

MATCHING UP WITH THE 1–3–1

Diagram 10-26 pictures the 1–3–1 starting positions. Generally, players 3 and 5 are the tallest defenders.

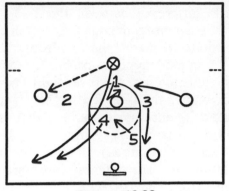

Diagram 10-22

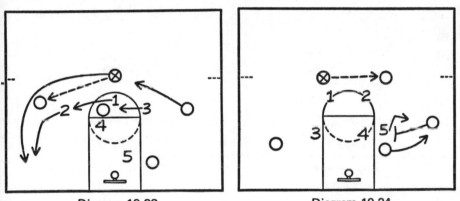

Diagram 10-23   Diagram 10-24

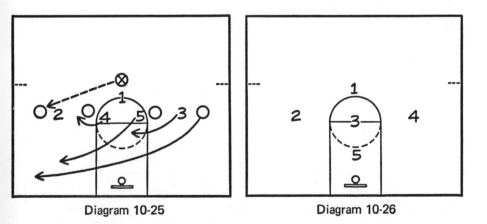

Diagram 10-25   Diagram 10-26

There is little difference between the 1—3—1 and 1—2—2 matching defenses. Each meets the one-front offenses matched out front and must rotate to match the two-front. The 1—3—1 has already put 3 and 5 in tandem positions, but the defense needs the tandem rule to be able to cover the rover and to cover the tandem post men when defending the 1—2—2 offense.

There are two different ways the 1—3—1 defense might rotate to cover the two-front offenses. They are:

1. Use the same rotations as in 1—2—2. The point man keys the rotation and the defense swings around with him. (Diagrams 10-27 and 10-28.)

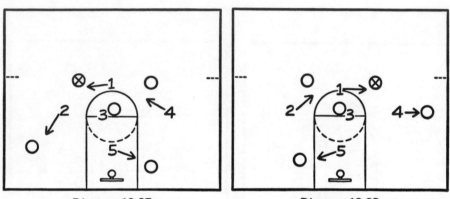

Diagram 10-27   Diagram 10-28

If both right and left rotation are used, it is necessary for the wing man to be able to use both guard and forward slides. (Diagrams 10-29 and 10-30.)

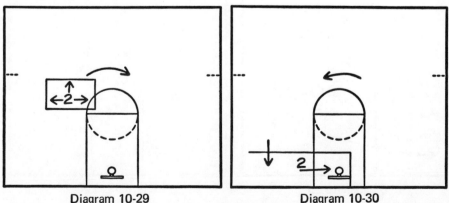

Diagram 10-29   Diagram 10-30

This rotation allows 3 to stay in the high post most of the time. He still might have to cover a corner on emergency occasionally. This method puts a heavy load on the wing men. Notice that 5 will cover either corner in double rotating because he moves opposite the point on the rotation.

2. The point and high post rotate to cover the two-front. Use the guards in spots 1 and 3 in this method. When a rotation is made 1 and 3 cover the guards in the two-front. Player 5 moves into regular post defense and the wings, 2 and 4, become back men. (Diagrams 10-31 and 10-32.) Only three men get much involved in rotating this way. If 3 is a tall or strong guard, he can often handle this spot well. The wings play only the wing and back spots, not at the guard. However, the guard must be able to defend in the post.

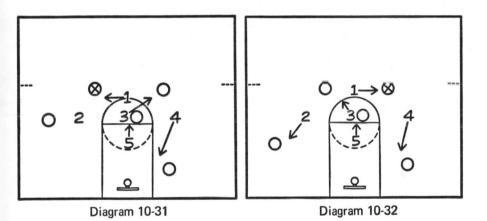

Diagram 10-31   Diagram 10-32

The slides for each position should be pointed out to all players. It depends on how the coach chooses to rotate as to which slides each position will have to make. The illustrations in the discussions of the 2−3 and 1−2−2 show the basic slides at the different positions. All of these may be applied to the 1−3−1 as the coach sees fit. The main difference in the 1−2−2 and the 1−3−1 is a matter of placing personnel. If the coach has two men who can play the back spots well, the 1−2−2 will be excellent. If he must limit the movement of one bigger man, he may go to

1–3–1 so that he only has the post slide and not the rover and back man slides. The slides are the same, it is just a matter of whom the coach selects to make them.

Using the Rules to Stay Matched

We will show three more zone offense moves to illustrate using the dribble and screen rules. In Diagram 10-33 the offensive wing dribble-pulled the defense to the corner. The perimeter defenders rotated with the ball and player 3 to cover the move. In Diagrams 10-34 and 10-35, 3 was screened and applied the screen rule to break up the play. He must take two steps up and one over in order to be effective.

All the moves we have used as illustrations can be used against the match-up. They would be covered the same way regardless of which alignment the defense began in. For this reason a team that knows the match-up rules can be a versatile zone team.

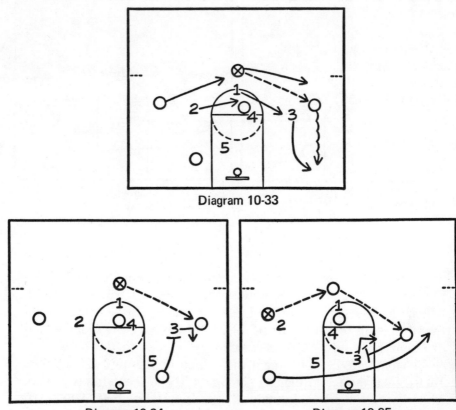

Diagram 10-33

Diagram 10-34   Diagram 10-35

LANING WITH THE MATCH-UP

After a coach understands the ideas of lane zoning (chapter 8) and of matching up he can use a forcing, laning defense with the match-up as well as the more conventional containing style we have been discussing. The slides, rules, and rotations remain constant. In match-laning one man must take the ballhandler; the players one pass from the ball match-up with the nearest men but move up to pressure the pass lane. The post men must move up to pressure their areas hard whenever the other men use laning tactics. By using a signal a defensive team can use the laning method off and on occasionally and cause the offense quite a bit of distress.

There are many different means by which a coach can have his team adjust in matching up. Once the coach understands the basic principles he may be able to improvise some change-of-pace techniques to give his match-up more versatility. For example, teams may delay matching up until after the offense makes a specific cut or when the ball goes to the wing area or on a signal by a player. We have tried to stay away from too many variations—just an adjustment or two to go to when an opponent exposed our weakness. We have employed a certain conservative option quite often. That is, since we advocate the multiple defense system we go into another defense when we cannot adjust to cover a particular offense satisfactorily in a game. We may go to a straight zone, to a lone zone, to man-to-man, or we might press. It may take some practice the following week to be able to cover the move that was bothering us. Regardless of the defense employed by a team as its basic one, there will be times when an opponent will get the better of it. But, all things considered, the matching zone is as good a choice for a basic defense as any available for most basketball teams.

Being able to use the match-up defenses has been a great asset to our teams. Since many coaches today do not teach the zone offense as well as they do the man-to-man we have been able to win some games we might not have pulled off with a man-to-man or a conventional zone. During some seasons we have used it as our main defense, while in other years we used it only as a change-up when we felt the opponent's zone offense had become rigid enough to allow a successful match-up quite easily. To be most effective with the match-up we have learned that it needs to be the team's basic defense because it takes a lot of practice time.

Teams who want to mix up defenses with an occasional zone should use conventional zones as discussed in chapters 7 and 8.

The match-up was our basic defense at Dale High School during an 18-4 season that found us ending the year with the second best defensive yield in the state of Indiana. We operated out of the 1–2–2 that year. We had three good defenders who played the point and the two back spots. Two sophomores who were not really ready for heavy defensive assignments at that time played the wings. We have since used the 2–3 and 1–2–2 match-up with higher-scoring and therefore more point-yielding Earlham teams with equal success in terms of wins and losses. But in years when the man-to-man was our basic defense we used conventional zones as change-ups once we learned that the match-up took a lot of time. Our suggestion for a coach who wants to use the zone as his basic defense is to go on into the match-up when he can.

HELPFUL HINTS TO REMEMBER IN PLAYING THE MATCHING ZONE

1. Pressure the ball in the scoring area.
2. Do not have two men on one offensive man unless a trap is ruled as an option in the defense.
3. Do not allow anyone to guard *open space*. Sag into the free throw area if a man has no one in his zone.
4. Use the option of allowing a wing man to get into the pass lane back out front when the ball goes to the corner occasionally. This should be used any time rapid ball movement seems to be hurting the defense.
5. Back men must constantly *turn their heads* to check the action behind them.
6. All players must *talk* constantly. In no way can this be *overemphasized.*
7. Block out each area around the basket for rebounding. Make the weak side front man move into rebound position behind the weak side forward. There should be two rebounders on the weak side.
8. All defenders must *slide hard* and fast to and from the ball.
9. Be *on* the ballhandler when he gets the ball. Give him no time to shoot.
10. Keep the inside area shut down—force it outside.

II

Drills for Teaching
Zone Defenses

Man-to-man defensive drills will help to build a better zone defense, but special emphasis should be put on the zone by using specific zone drills, too.

1. **Individual and Two-Man Drills**

    a.   Front man movement. Pass the ball back and forth several times. (Diagram 11-1.)

    b.   Front and back movement. Drill 1 getting the lane covered also. Pass back and forth. (Diagram 11-2.)

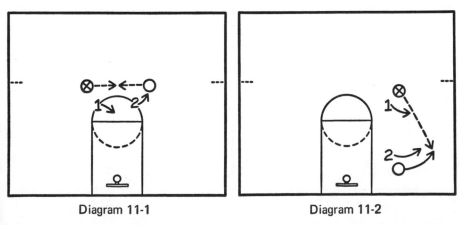

Diagram 11-1   Diagram 11-2

c.   Back man movement. (Diagram 11-3.)
d.   Use all five defensive players and allow no shots until 5–6 passes are made to check the movement.
e.   Back men head-turning drill. (Diagram 11-4.)
     The offense moves as they wish within the dotted area to get open; the back men must watch the ball and the offense. No shots allowed at first.

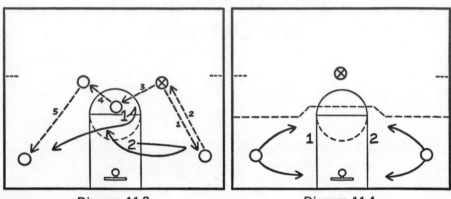

Diagram 11-3   Diagram 11-4

f.   Cutter practice for the individual. Do from front and wing. (Diagram 11-5.)
g.   Driver drill. Players take turns defending the drive. Others help out. (Diagram 11-6.)

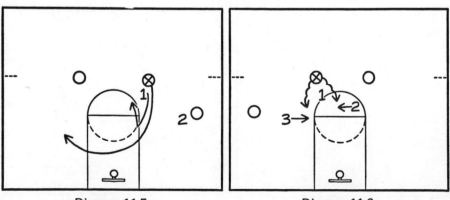

Diagram 11-5   Diagram 11-6

h.   Screen rule drilling. (Diagrams 11-7 & 11-8.)

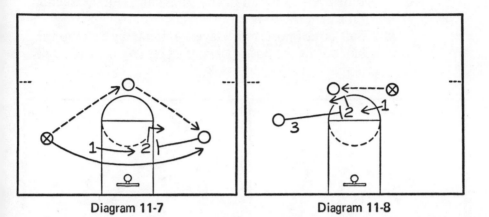

Diagram 11-7   Diagram 11-8

i.   By placing seven men around the perimeter and letting them pass the ball with no shots, the players can practice their slides individually, in pairs, or as a team. Chairs with numbers on them could be used instead of players. The coach can call the numbers out, indicating the location of the ball. (Diagram 11-9.)

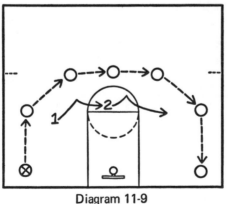

Diagram 11-9

j.   Post defense drill. Pass the ball around the outside. The post man tries to keep the ball out of the circled area. Players 3, 4, and 5 can rotate cutting in and out to make the post man work on cutters. This can be done until the ball is gotten inside 5 or 10 times. Also 2 or 3 defenders may be used. (Diagram 11-10.)

k. Ball out of post drill. Players 1 and 2 try to keep the ball out of the post. (Diagram 11-11.)

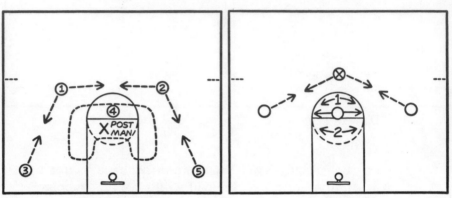

Diagram 11-10   Diagram 11-11

2. Lane Sliding Individual Work

a. Lane sliding individual work. 1 and 2 work on challenging the ball (can add post man). (Diagram 11-12.)

b. Front and back slides. 2 must cover wing and corner. (Diagram 11-13.)

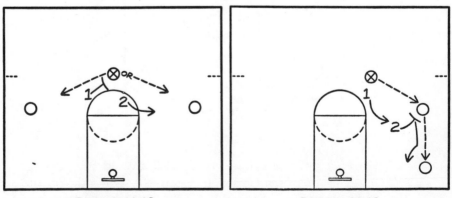

Diagram 11-12   Diagram 11-13

3.   **1–2–2 Front Slides**

2 or 3 move up to help 1 if they must and drop off as 1 gets to them. Pass back and forth (can add post man). (Diagram 11-14.)

4.   **Wing Lane Drill**

1 covers the wing and gets into the lane as the ball goes to the corner. (Diagram 11-15.)

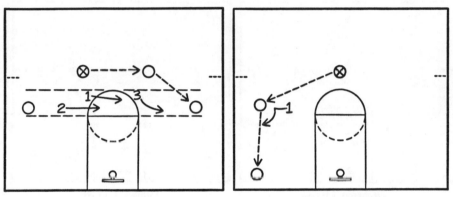

Diagram 11-14   Diagram 11-15

5.   **Wing-Corner Trap Drill (Diagram 11-16)**

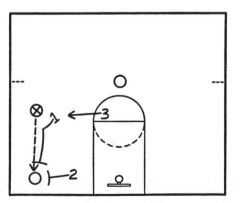

Diagram 11-16

6.   **Back Man Lane Drill**

Work on covering the low post. Reverse and play both sides (can add a high post man). (Diagram 11-17.)

7.   **Getting in the Middle of the Defense**

Pass the ball around the outside with no shots. Have each player touch the mid-point in the court when the ball gets two passes away. (Diagram 11-18.)

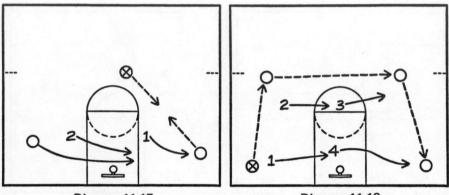

Diagram 11-17   Diagram 11-18

8.   **The Nine-Man Drill**

This teaches all match-up slides except the point moves. The ball is passed only from guard to guard. The defense covers the inside men as both they and the ball move. (Diagrams 11-19 & 11-20.)

9.   **Team Drills**

a.   The cutter to the goal rule. All offensive players pass and cut to the goal and pull out to the side opposite the ball. The ball is reversed side to side 4 or 5 times with no shots. (Diagram 11-21.)

b.   Wide cut to ball corner rule. Same process as 9a. (Diagram 11-22.)

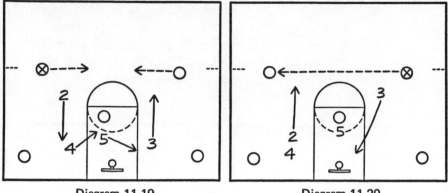

Diagram 11-19   Diagram 11-20

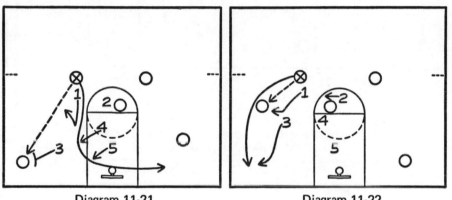

Diagram 11-21   Diagram 11-22

c. Deep cut to ball corner rule. Same process as in 9a.
    (Diagram 11-23.)

Diagram 11-23

d.   Dribble-pull rule. Same process as in 9a. (Diagram 11-24.)

e.   Screen rule. Same process as in 9a. Set screens on the front, wing, and back spots. Allow no shots. Diagram 11-25 shows only one example.

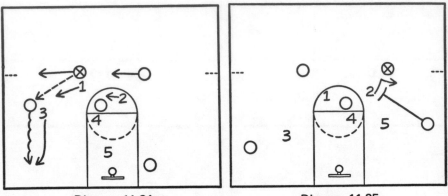

Diagram 11-24   Diagram 11-25

f.   Recovery drill. Same as the man-to-man Drill 13 in chapter 5. The ball beats each outside defender to the right and left. The adjacent defenders flex to help the ball defender recover. (Diagram 11-26.)

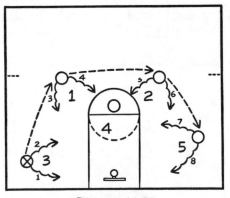

Diagram 11-26

g.   Trap drill at half-court. These traps (11-27 & 11-28)

are the same for man-to-man and zone. One trap shows the ballhandler turning his back on an adjacent defender and can be run on both sides of the floor. A coach may want to use other traps as well and will add them in on the drill.

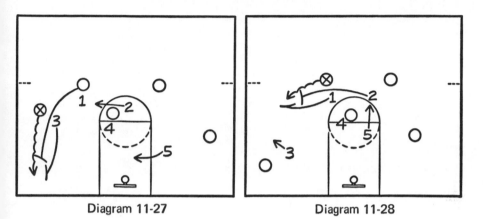

Diagram 11-27   Diagram 11-28

h.   Rover drill. Pass the ball around the outside. Let the two post men shift from high and low post to each corner. When one man stays in the high post the other defensive man on the tandem must rove the base. If the man 4 has drops to the low post, 4 will cover the corner and 5 will take the man 4 was defending. (Diagram 11-29.)

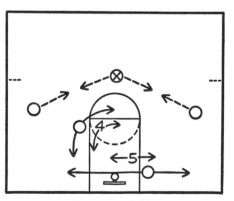

Diagram 11-29

i.   Ball in post drill. The offense passes the ball around the outside until it can throw to the post. Then the front men collapse on the ball and the post defender squeezes up. The other back men move in to protect the goal.

PART THREE

PRESSING DEFENSES

12

Developing the Individual for Pressing Defenses

The pressing defenses have reached a zenith of popularity in the past several seasons. Players like to play this style because it allows them to use their skills to the utmost. The players know the fans enjoy seeing this type of game, too. The press takes its toll from the poorly conditioned opponent, the slow teams, and the unsure ballhandlers. In general it puts the defending team on the attack. It increases alertness and is a fine spirit-builder. But the good pressing team must take a lot of pride in its defense because a good press is so devastating, while a poor one is spectacularly terrible.

It usually requires a good bench to press for lengthy periods of time, but any team should be able to utilize the press for certain situations. In the last minutes of a game in which the team finds itself trailing, a press is the best hope for victory. Just as important the press may be used at strategic times during the game when it might change the momentum of the game by giving the ball to the defenders, or by merely upsetting the opponent's offensive timing.

Foul trouble can prevent a team from using the press, but to say that a pressing team will automatically be a fouling team is not necessarily true. It often works out just that way, but if a team will concentrate on good habits in practice, it can reduce the foul dangers considerably.

A cool, collected offensive team can work the press over occasionally. The pressing team must be sure to keep the goal area protected to avoid allowing the morale-defeating lay-in most of the time. While it is true that the measure of a press's worth is not in the number of steals but in its total disruptive effect on the offense, there will be certain games in which the press will not be effective. Whether that be due to lack of mental preparation, tired legs, the offensive skills of the opponent or some other factor, it will happen. When it does the good coach will have the knack to know not to over-use the press.

It is interesting to keep in mind a point that has been proven many times. That is, if the press fails to accomplish the purposes of the coach in the first few minutes, the team may drop the defense for a time and then return to it later to find it effective. Or, many times a team will solve the press the first few times and then falter. This may be due to the adjustments the defense makes or the competitive nature of the defenders. The wise coach will not over-use the press when it is not paying off; neither will he give up in panic too quickly. If the press seems to be the proper defense, then observe, adjust, and try to ride it out for a while.

If the coach expects to use the pressure defenses much, he must prepare his team physically and mentally to be aggressive defenders. The players must accept the press as a part of their offense. To loaf or relax on the press will penalize the team in two important ways. First, the team spirit will sink if four boys work hard to pressure the ball but one prima-donna type loafs. He can negate all their work. Each player owes it to his team to do his best on defense at full court and half-court. The selfish player who refuses to do his part on the defensive end will ruin team morale. Second, the lax player will deprive himself possibly, certainly his team, of an offensive opportunity since the pressure defense is a part of the offense. We believe so much that the full court press is an offensive tool that we use an offense with quick scoring opportunities when we press. We believe that an offense which takes any time to set up will penalize the offense by breaking its momentum.

Either the man-to-man or the zone press may be used to accomplish the same purposes. The zone presses are usually more likely to produce steals but are also more risky, generally. Many man-to-man defenses are keyed to trap in certain situations which increase the ball-stealing opportunities with less overall risk than the zone defenses. By ruling the traps and teaching the keys, a coach can teach both the man-to-man and zone presses during the course of the season. In fact, when the coach teaches the similarities involved in the defenses, the same style of defense can be applied at full court, three-quarter court, or in only the front court. The main benefit of being able to do this is that the offense usually has to adjust more than the defense does to each change. The skillful defense will be able to make more adjustments than the offense.

Guarding the Ballhandler in Back Court

The defender should assume a wide base with both hands out, palms up. A wide stance will cause the defender to take a less direct path to travel forward. The answer to the question of how close to play is an easy one. Play as tightly as possible and still contain the ballhandler. Hard work will make this distance decrease gradually.

Playing the ball: When pressing man-to-man the man on the ballhandler will frequently have to guard the man one-on-one in the back court since most offensive teams will clear out for the ballhandler against this type of press. By trying to keep the body in front of the ball, "playing the ball," the defender hopes to make the ballhandler give up his dribble. Even if he fails to do this, he takes satisfaction in forcing the dribbler to turn his back once or preferably more in order to protect the ball. This gives the defender a victory because the dribbler might carry the ball or set himself up for a trap as he turns. Again, it may upset the offensive timing and that is a plus-factor for the defense.

Overplaying: The zone defenses usually require the man defending the ball to force it either inside toward the middle or to the outside toward the sidelines. The man-to-man presses may also ask for a particular overplay. In overplaying the defender must be sure to play close enough to give some pressure but must be sure not to allow the dribbler to get away from him very often. (See Drill 1 in chapter 11.)

Playing the Man One Pass from the Ball

Naturally, the presser will play close to and tough on the man only one pass away. The floor position will depend on the defensive plan. Some press styles will allow a pass into certain spots, then apply pressure. In this case the defender plays close to the defender but not so close as to risk allowing the opponent to back-door him.

The most normal defensive position would be to guard the man who is one pass away one step off of the pass lane or even in the pass lane itself. The defender will be closer to the ball than the offensive man—the distance depending on how far the offensive man is from the ball. The farther their distance from the ball, the farther the defender should play from his man in the direction of the ball. The man defending 3 is further from the ball than 2 in Diagram 12-1, for example.

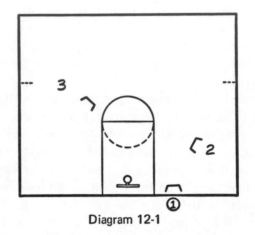

Diagram 12-1

The defender on 2 is one pass away and using the *closed stance* with the near hand in the pass lane. The closed stance will allow the defender to see his man better and will enable him to deflect passes occasionally. This stance is best when trying to keep the ball from a particular man. It is quite good to use this stance when the ball is out of bounds in order to cause a 5-second violation. The player on 3 is in an open stance due to his increased distance from the ball. Diagram 12-2 shows the open stance positions which are more conducive to stealing passes. The players open up toward the ball so they see the passes easier, but their man can slip behind them better than when the closed stance is used. The farther the offensive player is from the ball, the more successful the open stance will be. The most skilled pressers are able to use the open stance better and in more instances than can the poor defender. The coach must decide which stance to use; he may teach both successfully. (See Drill 2 in chapter 15.)

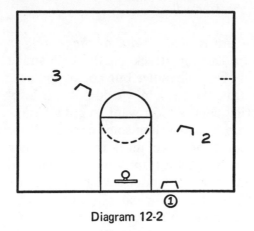

Diagram 12-2

Playing the Man Two Passes Away

As mentioned above, the further the presser is from the ball, the greater the distance should be between the defender and his assignment. Two passes away the open stance is best by far because it will enable the defender to pick off long or lob passes easier. The men two passes away must be ready to pick off passes, to recover for any front defenders who get beaten, to trap when possible and to protect the prime scoring area in any press defense. The open stance allows the defender to see more of the action so he can do his job better.

Guarding the Man Out of Bounds

If the defensive style requires guarding the man out of bounds, the defender waves his hands and yells at the ballhandler. Generally, the idea is to prevent the long bomb pass, so the best defensive position is with both hands high. If the hands are waving, the offense is less likely to try to thread a pass through them. The defender should also observe where the passer is standing regarding the basket overhead, if he is at the end of the court. If he is *under* it, he cannot pass high so the defender can concentrate to prevent the *short* pass. If the passer is to the left of the goal but close to it, he will be unable to pass high to the right side, etc. In general the defender should pressure the passing arm of the man out of bounds. (See Drill 3 in Chapter 15.)

Approaching the Ballhandler

When our team is *pressing out of the scoring area,* we ask for a *controlled approach* or attack on the ballhandler. We want to put pressure on the ballhandler but not to the point that we get beaten by the drive. To explain, we do not fear his shot since he is out of the scoring area. We do want to put on enough pressure to stop the easy pass, to cause him some concern. But we do not put on hard back-court pressure until the ballhandler gives up his dribble or else we put on a trap. We do *not* want the dribbler to get past or through our defenders. We must pressure, yet *control the dribbler.* Therefore we teach our players to move quickly toward the ballhandler but to begin to *spread out* and take shorter, controlled steps as they get close (5 feet or so) to the ballhandler out of the scoring area. The controlled steps with the wide, low stance help prevent the quick drive right past the defender. We call this "squatting out" at the ballhandler and it is a most important move. (See Drill 4 in Chapter 15.)

Recovering When Passed Up by the Ball

In pressing full court the defender tries not to get passed up by the ball. But it happens, so once a defender finds himself trailing the ball he must hustle to catch up to at least ball level. The player who watches the action from behind will not help the defense much.

When trying to recover to overtake a dribbler who has beaten him, the presser must pick out a cut-off point ahead of the dribbler and race to that spot, hoping to beat him there and regain a frontal position. (Diagram 12-3.) If he sees a back player coming up to trap with him, he would not try this, of course. He would form the trap with his teammate. He must never run along beside the dribbler and try to reach in and poke the ball. He must either get back in front or help trap if a teammate gets him stopped first. (See Drill 5 in Chapter 15.)

Playing the Passing Angles and Driving Angles in Traps

It is important for pressing teams to be aware of the passing lane—the line directly between the ball and the offensive man nearest the defender. Unless the defender is trying to keep his man from getting the ball at all the best policy is to be slightly back between the lane and the opponent's goal so as to make the lane *seem* to be open. If the defender will stand in a position between the ball and the man in his area, yet close enough to the man to catch a lob pass, the defender can entice the ballhandler to pass to the apparently open man and steal it. If the defender shows himself right in the lane, the passer is likely to look elsewhere to pass the ball.

Another good point to remember in playing for the pass is to observe the body and foot position of the man with the ball. If he *turns his back* to his defender, all the other defenders can afford to move up and get very aggressive. The man's pass options will be a short pass or a backward one. On the other hand, if the ballhandler *puts one foot in front of the other,* he is able to throw long, so the pass defense must give ground while the ball defender should pressure the passer.

If the defenders will try to keep aware of where the possible receivers are, more passes will be picked off. The defender who can see as much of the court as possible will make a better presser. A player must not watch the ballhandler only, unless his man has the ball.

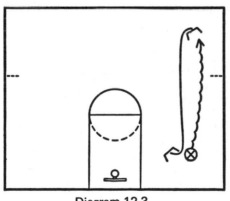

Diagram 12-3

How to Trap

The earlier discussion on trapping in chapter 3 applies to trapping in any defense. We should add here that the defensive team can afford to do more trapping down-court on screens, crosses and off-balance situations than in the half-court defenses. The reason, of course, is that a mistake down-court can be covered over before the ball enters scoring territory if the defense will hustle back. It is appropriate to emphasize a few additional points. A player must be sure to remember to keep the inside area closed off between him and his teammate when trapping so as to prevent a split. The angle is very important; try to set an outside trap as in Diagrams 12-4 and 12-5. The inside route is shut off by angling back and over. The players also use a "wedging" action toward the baseline as well, angling the ballhandler into the sideline.

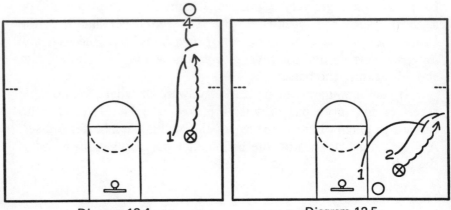

Diagram 12-4   Diagram 12-5

Never foul in a trap. The objectives in trapping should be to force a bad pass, deflect a pass with at least one finger, or get a 5-second call. Keep the hands back and up instead of reaching out to try to poke, slap or tie up the ball. Standing about two or three feet away from the ballhandler will also help prevent splits and fouling. Many defenders overcrowd in traps and lose their effectiveness.

Another important point to remember is that trapping is like stalking an animal. You can not make a big lunge at the man to set the trap while he still has a lot of room. He must be eased over and slowed down. When he is about corraled, put the clamp on. Trapping is quite an art. It takes aggressiveness, yet skill and patience. (See Drill 6 in Chapter 15.)

The Trapping Lanes

Observe how the court has been divided into three vertical lanes. (Diagram 12-6.) The reason for dividing the court vertically is to help players visualize the proper coverage when a trap is set as we did at half-court. In traps that occur in an outside lane a third man must cover the middle lane near the ball. The same lane as the trap but nearer the goal must be covered by a fourth man and the remaining man covers the middle lane basket area as they form the *defensive triangle* with the trap. (Diagram 12-7.)

In the traps that are sprung in the *middle* lane, the triangle is set by having the third and fourth men cover the two outside lanes near the ball and the fifth man protect the basket. (Diagram 12-8.)

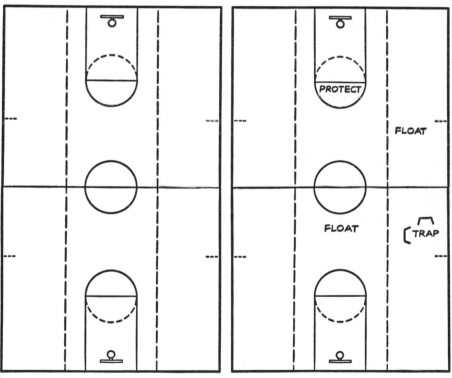

Diagram 12-6   Diagram 12-7

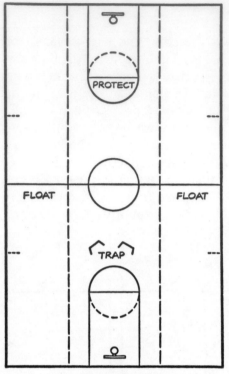

Diagram 12-8

Regardless of the type of defense, man-to-man or zone, the *trap coverage will always be the same.* Again, even in zoning with different alignments, the coverage is constant. In outside lane traps the "float" areas will be the flat pass in the middle lane and the down pass in the same outside lane. The last man will protect the goal. In middle traps, the two outside lanes around the trap will be floated by the first two who can get there and the goal must be covered. Thus, when players understand the principles involved here, they can react to traps in any defense. Even if they find themselves in a new position, drilling will acquaint them with the spots that must be covered. Trap and set the triangle! (See Drill 7 in chapter 15.)

Trap Areas

The best trap areas when the defense forces the ball to the *outside* are shown in Diagram 12-9. The eight corners provide the best spots. It may seem unusual to put in the spots just in front of the ten-second line in the back court. However, offensive players will many times stop before they get to the half line because they know they can get in real trouble if stopped just on the other side of that line. Anytime a dribbler stops to hunt people to throw to, he should be pressured hard or possibly trapped.

If the defense is forcing the ball to the *inside* the trap areas will be in the middle more like those in Diagram 12-10.

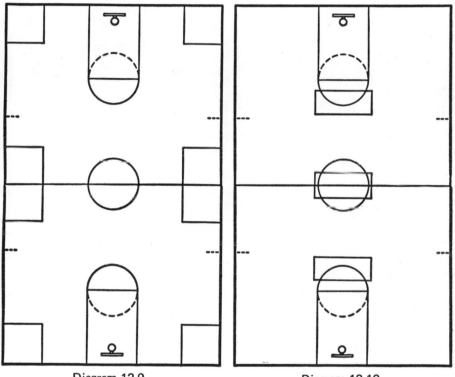

Diagram 12-9   Diagram 12-10

At times we will alternate pushing the ball in certain directions to add confusion to the offense. Or we may combine the overplays by forcing the ball one way in the back court, then using the opposite over-play in the front court. The latter tactics take a skilled defensive team.

Some teams have delineated the two overplays by the terms of "funnel" and "fan." The funnel defense would turn the ball into the middle, while the fan pushes the ball outside (Diagrams

12-11 and 12-12). They can alternate by having the guards yell one term or the other as the opponent takes the ball out of bounds. In using either of the fan or funnel defensive styles we usually allow the opponent to pass the ball in from out of bounds and then we push the ball in the preferred direction. This can be drilled using from one-on-one to five-on-five.

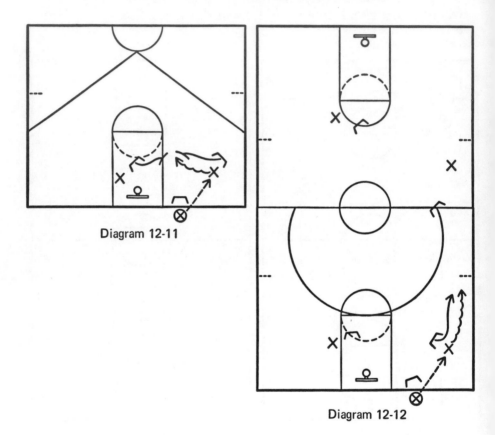

Diagram 12-11

Diagram 12-12

Rotating from the Trap

Another basic to pressing is the method of rotating. When the team is familiar with the techniques of setting a trap, the pass lanes and trap areas, they are ready to learn about rotations. Fortunately, rotating in any type or style of defense is almost as constant as the previous principles; therefore, learning the method of rotating in one defense will carry right over into another.

There are two rotations to make, *front* and *back*. Diagram

12-13 illustrates a trap in the outside lane. It makes no difference what type of defense is being played. As players 1 and 2 trap the ball, 3 and 4 float in the proper areas. Any one of three things may be done by the defense at this point. (1) They may hold positions and if the ball is successfully thrown out of the trap, 1 and 2 will scramble back into position to resume zone pressing or will get their men back again if playing man-to-man. Or, (2) the defense may rotate to the front. Diagram 12-14 shows 3 initiating a front rotation. We say that if he has a 50-50 chance to beat the reverse pass to the man, he should rotate up. A player can take either too few or too many chances on this. The man in this position must shut off the penetrating pass into the middle first of all, but if he never rotates up, he can get no steals. We like for the floater in the middle lane to check the middle and then be ready to rotate up to steal. If he senses the ballhandler may be trapped firmly, he can take more chances. As 3 rotates to steal, 4 must be alert. But, he cannot release from his area until the ball is reversed. If the ball is reversed, he rotates toward the area 3 left open. Here he must make a choice. If 5 is able to cover 3's vacated area or man, he will, and this puts 4 in the goal coverage position. If 5 cannot leave the goal, 4 will move all the way over to 3's spot. Player 2 will drop back hard just as the ball is thrown out of the trap. He will cover 4's area or man. Diagram 12-14 shows a complete front rotation. If 5 had been back too far to rotate up, an incomplete rotation would have been used to allow 4 to move over to cover 3's area or man.

(3) The other move the defense may use is the back rotation. This is why 4 could not give up his area until he saw the ball being reversed. Up until that time the ball might have been passed toward him. In the back rotation the ball is either dribbled or passed toward the player covering the down pass, 4 in Diagram 12-15. We use our back rotation any time 4 must cover the ball. The nearest man in the outside lane, 2 in our diagram, rotates back to trap with 4. The player in the middle lane floats that area. In the complete rotation, the goalie would move over to cover the down lane pass and the farthest diagonal player, 3, would move to cover the goal. Again, if 5 could not leave the goal, 3 would make an *incomplete rotation* and cover the down lane behind 4 for player 5.

To explain our use of incomplete rotations we say that our goalie will leave the basket area only if he feels the helpside man who is to cover the goal for him can make it to the goal in time to cover for him. After practicing it, the players will know when the factors of time and space allow a complete rotation. Remember, one of our basic principles is that we *cannot leave the basket unprotected.* (See Drill 8 in chapter 15.)

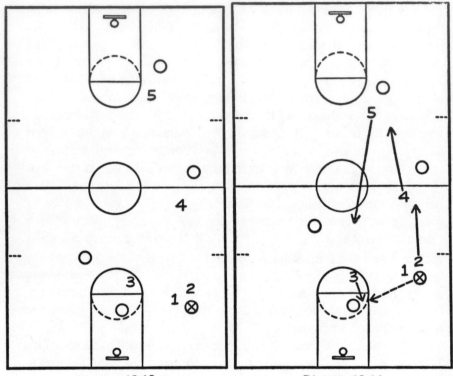

Diagram 12-13   Diagram 12-14

The two rotations are the same in man-to-man or zone. A slight difference may occur in timing if the coach so chooses. That is, he may allow rotations to be used *every* time a trap is set when playing man-to-man, for example. But we have found the 50-50 rule to be good for both defenses which makes them consistent.

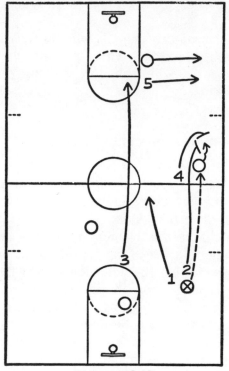

Diagram 12-15

Recovering Hard to the Goal

Whenever any press is broken the defense has a split second to avoid getting beaten. This is the most crucial moment in the press. Trappers must be drilled to blast back hard to adjust *every time* a ball is thrown from a trap. Every defender must be taught to catch up with the ball as soon as possible whenever the ball gets past them. So often we have gotten more steals in a game by running up behind the ballhandler and deflecting his dribble or stealing a pass to an apparently open man than on the original press. To make a really good recovery we tell all our players to funnel into the fifteen foot goal area whenever the ball beats us and then *build up our defense* quickly from there. They would get their proper men or zone spots after flooding the fifteen foot area. On sequence of coverage, we insist that they cover the goal first, the ball second, and then cover the remaining critical area, or men, near the ball, particularly the high post area. (See Drill 9 in chapter 15.)

The remainder of this chapter will illustrate how to use the principles described so far while pressing man-to-man. The following two chapters will show how the same principles can be used in zone pressing.

MAN-TO-MAN PRESS VARIATIONS

There are many ways to apply man-to-man pressure. There are certain aspects that are generally regarded as fundamental and we will mention these first. Most basic to the man-to-man press is *ball pressure*. Without this element there can be no successful press. By the same token men one pass from the ball must also be pressured. It is basic that the defender be near the pass lane and between the ball and his man. Players defending the help side two passes away must be sagged in ready to help in case the pressure is broken. The post areas must be defended very well to keep the ball out of this crucial area. The best man-to-man presses will allow for trapping and switching but these aspects will vary. Finally, the good pressing team will recover back very hard to protect the scoring area once it is beaten.

The Point of Initial Pressure

The same press can be changed from full court to half-court or three-quarter-court. Each change will often cause the offense a little bit of distress. In playing full court, sometimes we pressure the man out of bounds and sometimes we do not. When we do we hope to prevent the easy, calculated throw-in. It increases panic and enhances the prospect of a 5-second call. When we leave this man unmolested we use the freed man to float or to two-time either the best ballhandler or the first receiver he can find.

Generally, man-to-man teams that press the ball out of bounds will try to play the nearest offensive players very tough to force the throw-in to be a long pass, which is easier to steal. Coaches may select from different body positions to accomplish this. The defenders may do any of the following:

1. They may ignore watching the ball to assume *fronting* positions and concentrate on keeping between their man and the ball. (Diagram

12-16.) The defenders nearest the ball would be most likely to use this style of defense, although all the players could. (However, steals on long passes are more likely if the back men are open in such a way as to see the ball.)

2. The defense may play *beside* their men in a *closed* stance with the arm nearest the ball extended into or close to the pass lane. (Diagram 12-17.) This is probably the second best way to shut a man off from a pass.

3. The defense may play *beside* their men in an open stance with the hand farthest from the ball extended into or near the pass lane. (Diagram 12-18.) This style is a little more risky but will usually produce more steals.

4. The defender may play *behind* his man and try to force him into a specific area or trap situation after he gets the ball.

5. The defense, particularly deep men, may play well in *front* of their men, but open and facing the ball. (Diagram 12-19.) This may yield a long pass and lay-in occasionally but provides more steals and more helping out.

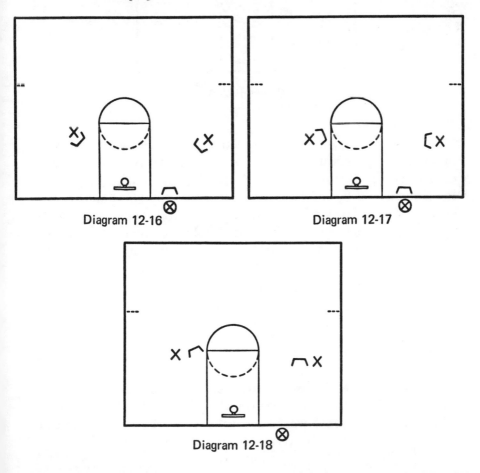

Diagram 12-16   Diagram 12-17

Diagram 12-18

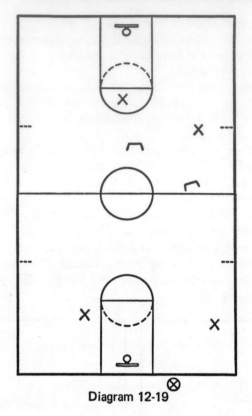

Diagram 12-19

The coach may use any one of the above styles for all his men or he may rule his defense so that the players use, for example, *closed front* in the area marked A in Diagram 12-20, *open beside* the man in area B, and *open front* in areas C and D so long as the ball is out of bounds or in area A. Naturally, and other combination might be selected. The labeling of the lateral areas of A, B, C, and D saves a lot of words when communicating with players. The coach may with little adjusting instruct his players to change from a full court press to three-quarter court by telling the guards to pick up the ball in the B area. Or he may go to the half-line press by calling for pressure at C. He may also label the man-to-man and zone aspects with a number or name and save further communication time. A few seconds count a lot in time outs.

Most pressure defense coaches feel that the half line must be challenged by the defense against the initial offensive thrust so that a pressing defense would generally be an A, B, or C point of pressure. The team would then recover into the specified style of defense at D, the scoring area. This D defense may well be a press, the same defense as used to meet the ball at A, B, or C. Or, the D defense may be a more conservative, basket-protecting defense. It all depends on what the coach wants to do with his defense.

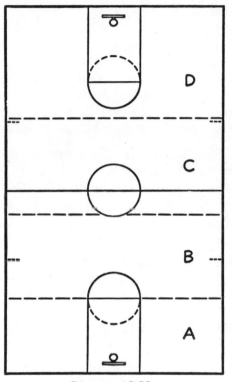

Diagram 12-20

Overplays

The coach will have to choose whether to overplay the offense outside to push the ball to the middle, inside to push the ball to the side lines, or to play straight away on each man in an attempt to play the ball only. In the latter case the defender would play the ball and try to turn it away from the direction it would be going at that time. The type of overplay used will help determine the kind of traps that will occur and the places where they might be applied.

Switching

As mentioned in our earlier discussions on switching the coach has a wide choice of possibilities. (Chapters 3 and 4.) Coaches usually decide to allow more switching in the presses longer than half-court than they do the half-court only presses. There is so much area to cover, it is harder to stay with one man. The coach may decide to:

1. Avoid switches.
2. Allow switching on every screen.
3. Allow switching on all screens *and crosses.*
4. Switch on screens in certain areas (such as A and B) with all players.
5. Allow only his guards to switch. This could be on crosses and/or screens in certain areas, or all over the court.
6. Stay with the same rules as in his half-court ruled defense.

In general the coach will have a better defensive team when he can correlate the half-court and full court defensive rules. Consistency in switch rules is very important. One common rule we use is to allow switching between guards on screens and crosses in *all areas;* and to switch on all successful screens for everyone else all over the court. With some teams we have found it necessary to change the last aspect of the rule, at the risk of having a heavier teaching load.

WHEN TO TRAP WITH THE MAN-TO-MAN

As mentioned in previous discussions on trapping, certain keys are necessary so the defense will know when to anticipate a trap. Some coaches will limit traps to specific spots on the floor, some will key to certain situations. These situations are usually any or all of the following:

1. On the guards screen or cross move allowing both defenders to jump the ballhandler.
2. When the ballhandler turns his back on a possible trapper.
3. When the ballhandler is stranded with all of his teammates in front of him, as in a clear-out at full court particularly.
4. When the ballhandler is off-balance.
5. When the dribbler is forced into a second defensive player. (Diagrams 12-21 and 12-22.)

The trap techniques are the same as have been described

earlier. It is well to add that the difference in trapping man-to-man or zone is that the keys vary. The zone will force more traps generally, while the man-to-man will trap on one of the key situations. It is a matter of difference in timing.

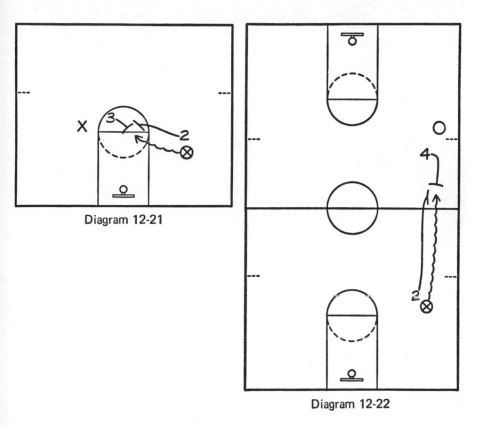

Diagram 12-21

Diagram 12-22

Specific Man-to-Man Trap Situations

In Diagram 12-23 the ballhandler drove hard toward the side and in so doing turned his back on player 2, who ran to trap with 1. Immediately players 3 and 5 jump to float the two pass lanes and 4 is ready to cover the goal. Incidentally, if the ball gets past everyone else, 4 must zone the basket area, letting his man go, until he can get some help from his retreating teammates.

In this situation 3 may rotate to steal or if the ball is thrown toward 5 a back rotation might be used. If no rotation is used 1 and 2 would scramble to get their men back. Diagram 12-24 shows a front rotation.

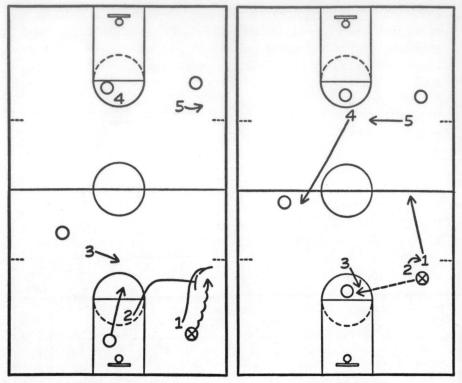

Diagram 12-23   Diagram 12-24

The guard-forward or front-back trap to the *outside* slides are shown in Diagram 12-25. The same coverage must be made as in the guard-guard trap to the outside, although different players cover the vital areas. Players 2 and 5 set the trap while the triangle is set as 4 covers the outside down-court lane, 3 gets the goal covered, and 1 protects the middle flat pass area. This is a back rotation. All players must be alert to perform these moves quickly. If 5 comes to trap, he must keep his hands high and has to be able to get to the ballhandler in a hurry. To react slowly will give the ballhandler an opportunity to throw over 5's head and will put a lot of pressure on the basket. Obviously 4 must be alert to move as 5 goes to trap. But most crucial is the long slide 3 must make. The *third man has to run hard toward the goal when a back man gets into a trap.* Player 4 cannot rotate unless he feels 3 will cover the goal. This principle will hold true in all press combinations. Had the trap been set by players 3 and 4 on the other side of the floor, player 2 would have been the third man while 5 and 1 would have floated into the crucial pass lanes. The "third man" is always the weak side front man in outside traps, the man covering the flat pass lane. On inside traps the third and fourth men get the outside lanes and the fifth man covers the goal. Diagram 12-26 shows the guard-forward inside trap which occurs less often than other traps. Whenever the ball is thrown into the middle right over the out of bounds defender's head he should retreat hard right toward the ball. This is a hard pass on the defense. Player 4 would try to prevent his man from getting the ball in this area, but at times it will happen anyway. If 1 and 4 can trap, 2 and 3 float the outside lanes and 5 covers the goal. If the alignment of the offense were off-balance the defense has to use its knowledge of the three lanes to know where to cover. (Diagram 12-27.) Players 1 and 4 trap. The right outside lane has no defender so 5 is the closest player to that lane and must rotate to it if the trap is set, provided there is an offensive player in that lane. Player 2 covers the left outside lane and 3 protects the goal.

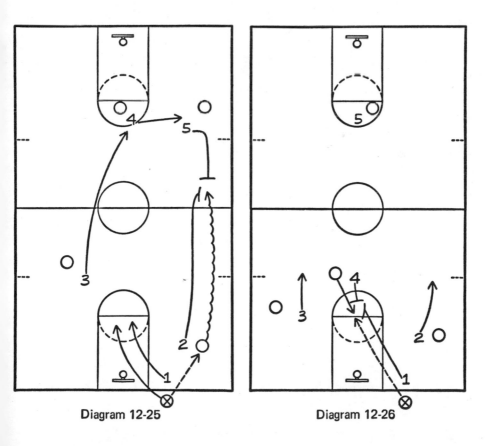

Diagram 12-25   Diagram 12-26

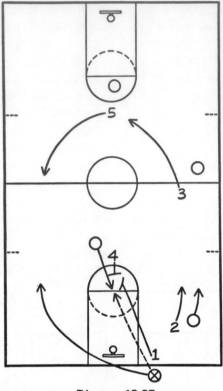

Diagram 12-27

The guard-to-guard trap when *forcing inside* or funneling is shown in Diagram 12-28. It should be understood that when we use the term "guard-to-guard" that in reality these players may not actually always be guards, only playing in front positions at the time, but we will continue to use the terms of guard and forwards as well as front men and back men.

The inside trap is set by 1 and 2. Since 3 is in one outside lane and the other is uncovered, 5 moves up to cover the outside lane and 4 plays goalie. In Diagram 12-29 players 2 and 3 form the trap and since 1 is in the left outside lane, 4 covers the open outside lane and 5 gets the goal assignment.

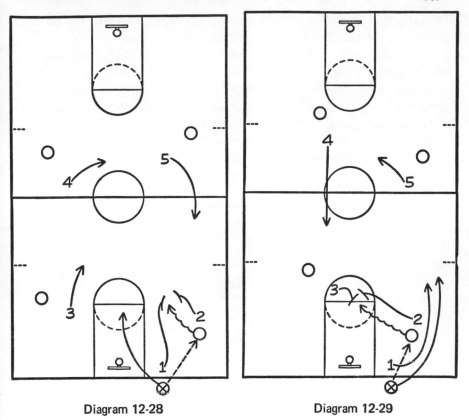

Diagram 12-28   Diagram 12-29

Rotating from a middle lane trap is very simple. If the ball is thrown toward the opponent's goal the defense must merely scramble to recover. If the ball is thrown to either outside lane, the nearest trapper and floater go to the ball while the rest of the defenders adjust to cover the proper lanes. Diagram 12-30 shows 1 and 2 forming a middle trap. Players 3 and 4 cover the outside lanes and 5 has the goal. As the ball is thrown to the outside, 1 and 3 go to the ball while 4 and 5 follow the rotation toward the ball. These are the same slides as the front rotation discussed before. If the pass were thrown in 4's direction out of the trap, the rotation would go the same way in the opposite direction, of course.

The slides on the full court press are the same at three-quarter and half-court. As was noted earlier in the chapter on "Team Man-to-Man Defense" and again in the zone defense traps there is one more trap possibility, the deep-post forward-forward, or forward-post trap. We will not cover this again now but the same lane coverage principles may be applied.

A team that understands how to trap, cover the passing lanes, and to rotate in the man-to-man can make the transition to zone pressing quite easily. The man-to-man press is a bit more conservative and, therefore, safer than the zone press. But when a team can use both, they can go into whatever type the situation demands. The next two chapters will show the basic similarity between the man-to-man and zone presses.

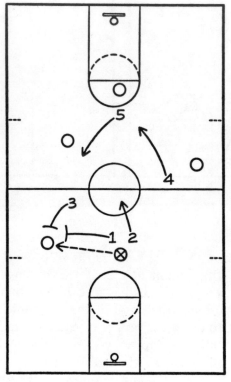

Diagram 12-30

13

Coaching the
Matching Zone Press Defense

We have had a great deal of success with the match-up zone press over the past few seasons. Our overall quickness has served to great advantage in the press at full court, but when our speed was not so great we were able to use the same slides at three-quarter or half-court. Although there have been times when we tried to get away from the press as our key defensive weapon, we have always come right back to it. No defense has been so devastating and momentum-bearing for us as the press. From the time when our first little junior high team broke the 100 point barrier three times until Earlham College became nationally ranked sporting a 100-plus per game season offensive average, the press has been our defensive bread and butter. We may begin the game pressing or we may come in with it at a later point. But very few games end without our having pressed full court. The game situation usually will call for it unless we get in a runaway in our favor. The players and fans love it. In high school our fans even helped us out by roaring loudly when our boys caught an opponent in a trap.

The press has gotten our teams off to a good start on many occasions. Pressing tends to relax a team and adds to the apprehension of the opponent in the opening minutes of the game. It has often given our teams the "gap-time" it takes to break a game open. There are many instances in which we have scored from ten to twenty points while holding our opponent nearly or completely scoreless in the process due to the press. We will always remember winning a game in regulation time in which the clock showed only thirty-seven seconds remaining to be played with our team down seven points and it was the other team's ball out of bounds. Teams without the press as part of their defensive system are seriously handicapped. The press can change the game complexion like nothing else can.

Basic Alignment in the Match-up Press

The beginning formation is a 1-2-1-1 alignment. These only serve as starting points since the defense will adjust or match with what the offense attempts to do. Bear in mind that the defense matches up until the ball is thrown in, then must begin to concentrate on leaving their men in order to trap. (Diagram 13-1.) As soon as it is the opponent's ball the defensive players race to these general areas and then match-up along the following guidelines. Note that there are restrictions in the match-up. We do not *always* get exactly matched up because of the zone demands to keep the trap lanes covered. Normally we are able to match-up, however.

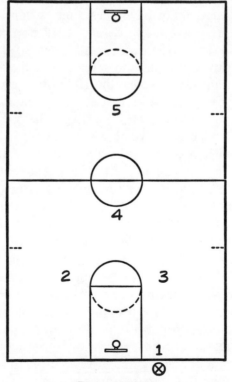

Diagram 13-1

Player 1 tries to get to the man out of bounds right away to slow the offense down and give his teammates time to match with the offense. Occasionally the point man will not take the man out of bounds and instead will try, to two-time one of the in-bound players. This is a good variation. When he does this, all players try to shut off their man in order to force a 5-second out of bounds call or a "panic-pass." Another variation for the point man is to check the man out of bounds only momentarily, then drop quickly to jam up the middle until he can trap.

The original positions of the wing men, 2 and 3, are about two or three steps behind the foul line extended and a step or two from the foul lane. (Diagram 13-2.) These are only starting positions from which to adjust. The wing men quickly look around to find their men. Player 3 will take the first man toward the ball in the quarter-court area to the left of the point man. (Diagram 13-3.) Regardless of matching up, unless we call for a special move, he will *not* cross the vertical middle of the floor as long as the ball is still out of bounds in order to keep that lane covered. If there is no one in his area, he will drop straight back as far as the half-line to find a man until the ball is thrown in and wait to see what develops. The basic thing to learn in the initial line up is that the wings generally allow the first pass in-bounds, but they try to force the offensive players in their area down toward the end line so the ball will be thrown in *as close to the end line* as possible. (Diagram 13-4.) This sets up an early trap situation and is a hindrance to the return pass to the man coming in from out of bounds.

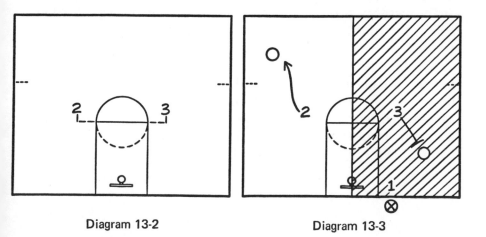

Diagram 13-2   Diagram 13-3

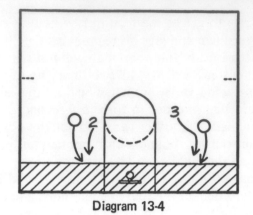

Diagram 13-4

Player 2 on the other wing side has the same responsibilities as 3. He will take the first man to the right of player 1. There may be special times in which we will allow a violation of the basic slides and coverage, but these general match-up rules apply in nearly all situations, regardless of their simplicity.

Player 4, the middle man, must be an alert basketball player. He must *observe the player movement* in front of and behind him. He must be a good anticipator and it helps if he has good speed and hands. He starts at the half-line area in the middle of the court and adjusts toward the overloaded area lining up with the fourth offensive player. (Diagrams 13-5 and 13-6.) Once the pass comes in, he will adjust to the side the ball is on and will keep adjusting as the ball is passed or dribbled from side to side paying attention still to the fourth offensive player. He must gradually fade back as the ball progresses up the floor toward the basket, too. (Diagram 13-7.) Another key point is that the 4 man must prevent the in-bounds pass right up the middle. He will go only as far as the dotted line in Diagram 13-8 to prevent the pass, however. If the offensive cutter goes past that, the defender would get back fast to his starting position. The other three front men will be able to absorb him if the ball is thrown to him in the lane.

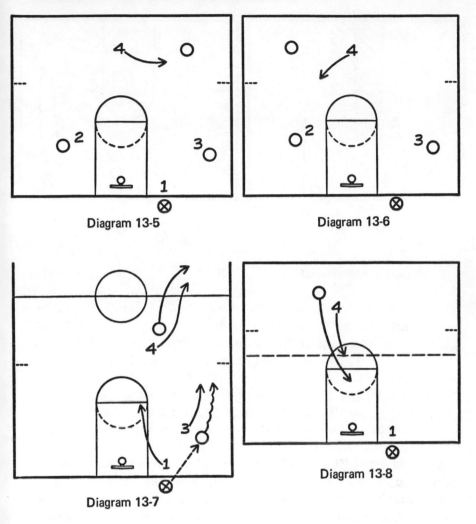

Diagram 13-5

Diagram 13-6

Diagram 13-7

Diagram 13-8

Player 5 is the "goalie" and must protect the goal area. He takes the fifth offensive player. It is his prime responsibility to prevent the lay-in. His normal move is to drop straight to the basket as the ball progresses toward the goal rather than to worry about matching up, once the ball is in play. If he needs to cover a man in the corner, he may do so *provided* one of the men coming from the weak side yells to him that he will cover the goal for him. (Diagram 13-9 and 13-10.)

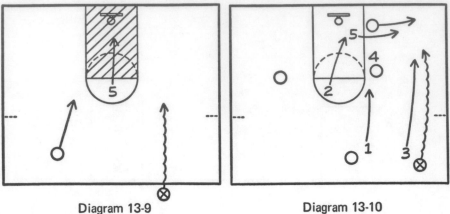

Diagram 13-9   Diagram 13-10

Placement of Personnel

When the defense is spread over the court it is helpful to have five good athletes. It is difficult to hide anyone who cannot play well. Each man must do his job or the whole effort will fail. The *point man* must either be a quick-moving, sure-handed guard or a mobile big man. The advantage of the tall player is obvious for trapping and for long pass protection. The wing men may be guards or forwards or one of each. Their moves are not difficult but *must be executed perfectly.* Precision at the wing is vital to forming traps, preventing splits, rotating to steal, or recovering for the middle man. The middle man must be a good "reader" of the offense. He may be a guard, but it is better for him to be a forward. The goalie may be a guard or the center. If he is a guard, he may be able to get up and down the floor quicker than the center, since the center must run from end line to end line. He can help conserve the big man's energy and fouls. But if the center is not a quick enough man to play the point, he may not fit into the defense anywhere but at goalie. One real advantage of having the center at goalie is that much of the time he can help prevent lay-ins just by his presence. This is reason enough for using a tall goalie.

General Principles

Before discussing the specific movement of the defenders we should set forth the basic principles in the press. First, they try to match-up with the offense and to keep a three-man front on the ball. If they send only two men, we force them to bring a third by fronting the second man. The fourth man lines up with their fourth man and is the floater to check the down-court passes, serving as a back-up man for the three-man front. Second, the three front men try to force the ball to either of the outside lanes. They want to push the ball to the outside, then trap. If they steal, that ends the defensive effort, of course. (We only make a few steals in some games but feel a press can still be very effective without steals. Steals are extra.) When they do not get a steal, they try to recover in such a way as to re-form the three-man front. They then try to push the ball back to the outside and trap again. (Diagrams 13-11 and 13-12.) They do this until the offense gets the ball past the trap area in mid-court. (Diagram 13-13.) The idea is thus to *match-up, push the ball to a side,* and *trap* when possible. If the offense escapes, try to recover in order to push the ball to the side and trap again.

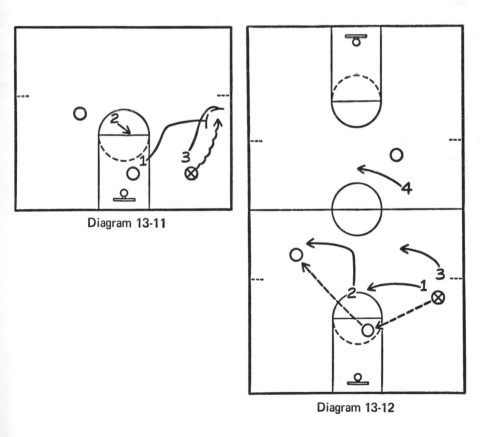

Diagram 13-11

Diagram 13-12

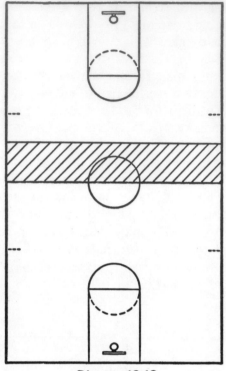

Diagram 13-13

Rotation to Steal

After a trap is set, the two floaters who get the crucial pass lane area must decide whether to try to steal or not. If one moves to steal we must *rotate our defense toward him* in case he fails to get the steal. As always there are two rotations in our basic outside traps, the front rotation and the back rotation. Observe the front rotation in Diagrams 13-14 and 13-15. Players 1 and 2 are trapped.

Player 3 floats to the middle lane. He has to decide whether to stay in the middle and *protect* conservatively or to try to *rotate* and steal. If he sees the ballhandler get in trouble and feels he has a 50-50 chance, he will move up ready to steal. After player 4 sees the ball reverse directions, he reverses, too. But he *cannot* rotate up *until* the ball is reversed. If 3 had intercepted, he would have two points. If he failed, he would need help. This is where the rotation comes in. The 4 man moves up to the outside lane and the outside trapper on the ball, player 2, drops back hard to cover 4's area. We would ideally have a three-man front again now after the rotation. This same move can be used on the other side of the floor, of course. While we want to rotate to steal when we can, we want to have a fair chance of getting the ball if we do rotate. To rotate carelessly will open up the crucial middle area behind the man rotating to steal. (Diagram 13-16.) Note that the rotation is the same as in man-to-man pressing (chapter 12).

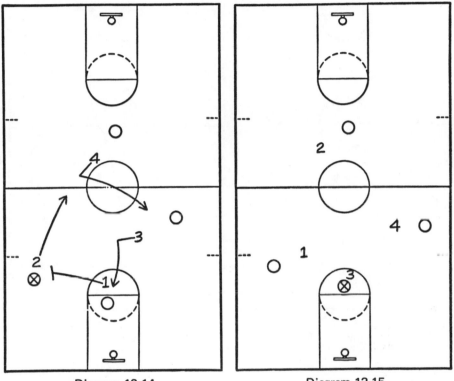

Diagram 13-14   Diagram 13-15

The back rotation is shown in Diagrams 13-17 and 13-18. If the ball is thrown down the outside lane, 4 must cover the ball. Or, if 4 decides to come to trap with one of the wing men, the same rotation is necessary. *Anytime* the fourth or *middle man covers the ball,* the opposite side *wing man must rotate* back to cover. This is the back rotation. Observe in the diagrams how the players rotate so that we still have a three-man front with a fourth back-up man. The new three-man front would try to keep pressing until the offense gets past the mid-court trap area. If the goalie can rotate up, he will. If he cannot leave the goal, only the four players will rotate. Again this is the standard back rotation.

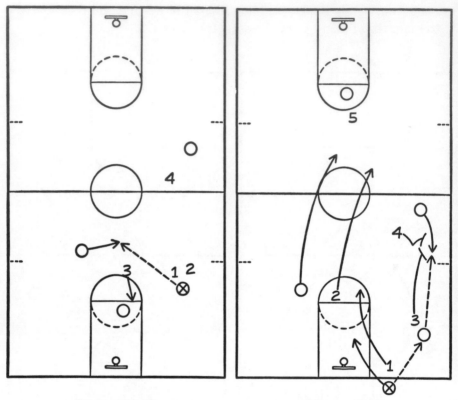

Diagram 13-16   Diagram 13-17

In summary on the principles, we *match-up, push* the ball to the outside, *trap* when we can, then *rotate* to steal if possible. If they keep possession we try to form a new three-man front, push to the side and trap again until they get past their mid-court. If there is no rotation to try to steal, we keep the same three men in position trying to push the ball to the sides. It is easy to understand why we do not want the ball dribbled or passed through the inside of our defenders—we plan to push the ball outside. We will give attention to covering this mistake when it happens later.

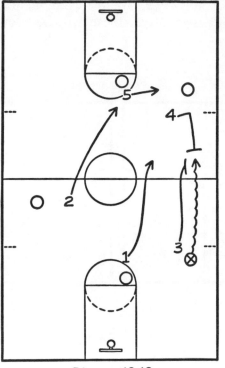

Diagram 13-18

Basic Slides in the Press

The *point man,* player 1, will *move back* quickly a step or two as soon as the ball is thrown in and then make one of three moves. (1) He may just hold up and bide his time for the moment until he feels he can get into a good trap. He can help prevent a quick return pass to the man coming in from out of bounds by doing this, too. This is a good move when the opponent has used this pass a few times. (2) He can go immediately over to the ball and trap. He will do this most often, especially if the wing men are successful in pushing the in-bounds receivers down toward the end line enabling the point man to trap quickly. (Diagram 13-19.) If the point cannot get to the trap in a hurry, he is better off to drop back and stay in the middle lane waiting for a better trap situation. Or (3) the point man must race straight backward when the ball is successfully thrown in-bounds directly over his head up the middle lane. (Diagram 13-20.) These are the basic moves of the point man; if he masters them he can play a good press game. There are other special moves we give the point man occasionally to cover specific offensive plays, these will be shown in the next chapter.

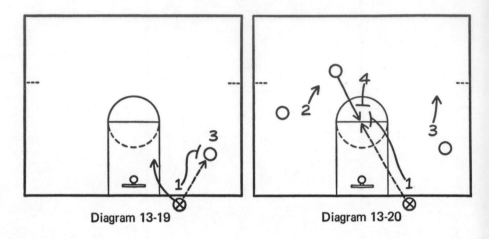

Diagram 13-19   Diagram 13-20

It is important that the point man *angles back first* and then over to the ball when he traps so he can help shut off the dribbler's inside drive. (Diagram 13-21.) We do not want our trappers split. Remember that the point man does not *automatically* go to trap the ball; he goes at the opportune time. Sometimes the right moment is immediately, especially when the throw-in is a very short one; otherwise the trap may not come for a few seconds. Drilling will teach the proper sense. (See Drills 6-9 in chapter 15.)

The *wing men,* players 2 and 3, have different responsibilities, depending on whether we are trying to steal the first pass or to allow the first pass to come in-bounds. If we call out, "first pass" (usually we will have our point man tell the other two men), the wings use a closed stance on their men and get as much between the ball and the man in their area as possible in order to prevent the first pass in. To force a bad pass is the idea.

Normally we allow the first pass to go in. But we do not just sit back and allow it to be thrown in wherever the offense wishes. The wings get in position beside the first man toward the ball in their area and force them up close to the end line. Then they let up so as not to be back-doored. (Diagram 13-22.)

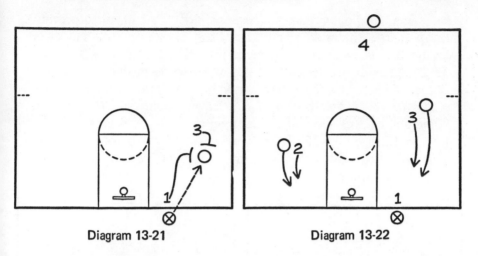

Diagram 13-21   Diagram 13-22

If the ball is thrown in to the man the wing is covering, he should put pressure on him but not enough that the ballhandler will be able to drive past him. He must push the driver outside so he overplays the inside. (Diagram 13-22.) He will try to contain the dribbler until either 1 or 4 traps with him or the man passes the ball. He will have to angle or "wedge" the ballhandler toward the sideline to prevent a split and to keep him contained. He should approach from an *inside angle* so as to prevent an inside drive and spread out his legs to control his speed on his last two steps as he nears the ball in order to keep the man from driving past him. Diagram 13-23 shows the inside angle approach.

If the ball is thrown in to the side opposite the wing man, this weak side wing man becomes a floater. (Diagram 13-24.) The weak

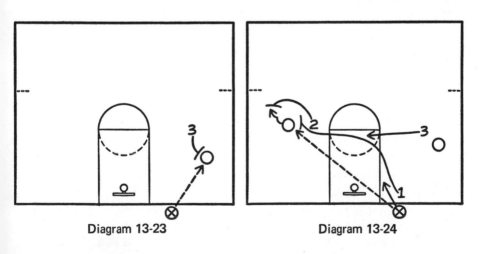

Diagram 13-23   Diagram 13-24

side man, or floater, has the responsibility first of all to prevent
the pass into the middle lane just ahead of or even with ball level.
If the ball is successfully thrown into the shaded area (Diagram
13-25, he controls the ballhandler and tries to push him to a side.
If the ball is thrown back to 1's man and reversed up 3's side, he is
ready to *cover that outside lane.* He must not run to the ball.
(Diagram 13-26.) See how all the men move as the ball escapes the
trap in Diagram 13-26. There was no attempt to rotate so they
scramble back. This is the basic move for outside lane traps, when
no rotation occurs.

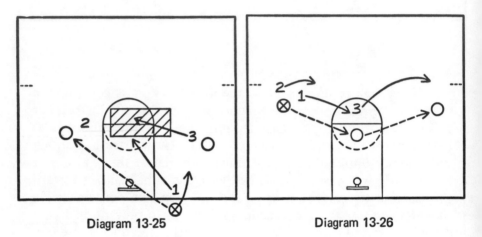

Diagram 13-25   Diagram 13-26

The *second responsibility* of the weak side wing man is to
anticipate a rotation to steal. If he covers the middle, the man in
the trap will likely throw either down-court in his same outside
lane or will pass backward. If the ballhandler *turns his back* to the
trappers, he will not likely throw ahead down the outside lane.
Therefore, when this happens the wing man can sense a possible
steal rotation for the backward pass. He must be ready to rotate
up to steal a reverse pass anytime; likewise he must be ready to
rotate back to cover on the back rotation for the middle man
whenever that man gets in play on the ball. Diagram 13-27 shows
the front rotation for the wing man's steal and Diagram 13-28
again shows the back rotation due to the middle man's move to
the ball.

One critical point must be re-emphasized regarding the weak
side wing's play that takes some time to learn. In the case where
the wing decides *not to rotate* to steal and the ball is reversed, he
must *not rush* to the ball in the middle lane. He waits for 1 to
recover to the ball and tries to protect his own outside lane as a

Diagram 13-26. Only if the driver drives up the middle right at 3 can he afford to take him. Then he does so only to slow the offense down to allow the defense to get back.

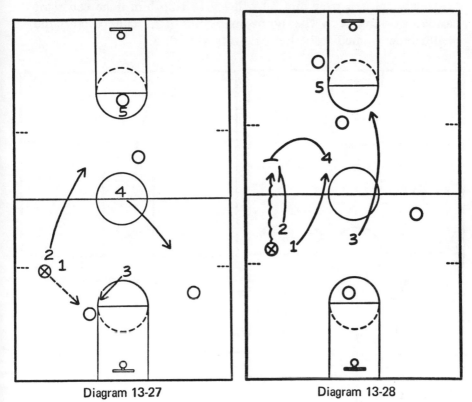

Diagram 13-27   Diagram 13-28

If the offense puts only two men down to bring the ball up court, the wing man guarding no one moves back toward the half-line until he finds a man. The wing guarding the in-bounds man tightens up on his man to help force a third offensive man into the play (Diagram 13-29). The reason we do not allow the wings to cross the dotted line when the ball is out of bounds is so we will have all three lanes covered initially. If a wing has no one in front of him and forgets to drop back, 4 must yell to him for help at the half-line. We must match-up, yet still keep a three-man front.

The *middle man* will take the fourth offensive player while the ball is out of bounds and then cover the half-line area toward the ball side when the ball progresses up the floor. He tries to stop the half-line pass and to cover any cutter coming from the half-line into the middle lane area in the back court up to about the foul circle, as mentioned earlier. (Diagram 13-30.) If the cutter continues on past the foul circle toward the ball, the middle man backs off to his original spot. The three front men should be able to cover the front area adequately. If the ball is thrown to the cutter while 4 is near him he will try to trap him if he can right away, working with the point man. But if he cannot stop the ballhandler immediately, he *must* retreat with 5.

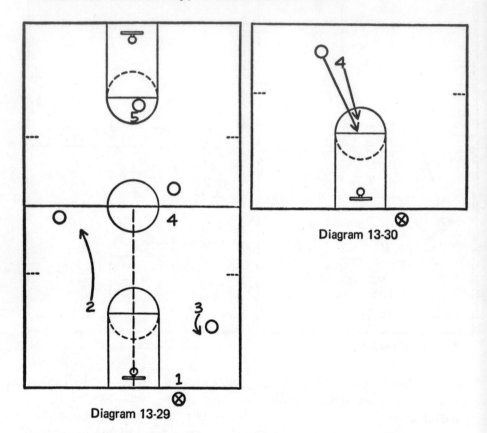

Diagram 13-29

Diagram 13-30

After the ball is thrown in-bounds 4 will float for the forward pass threat, generally in the outside down lane. He will try to be the back up man for the three-man front. Therefore, he will move just as the ball moves from side to side. As important as this *lateral* movement is his *vertical* movement. That is, as the ball progresses up court he must gradually give ground to be able to protect the scoring area with the goalie.

The middle man must be ready to steal the down-court pass or to trap with a wing man in the outside lane if the ballhandler gets past the wing. He hopes to put on this trap just as the ball crosses the half-line, but must be ready to go sooner if the ballhandler stops. Diagram 13-31 shows the middle man stopping the pass, while Diagram 13-32 shows him trapping a dribbler. These are back rotations.

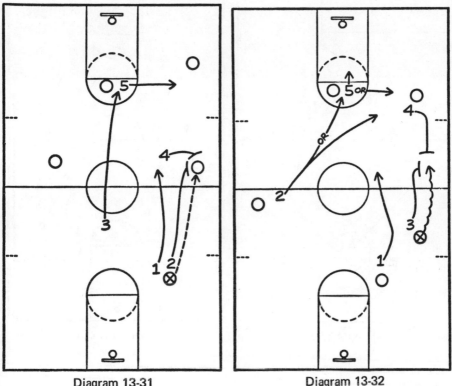

Diagram 13-31   Diagram 13-32

The middle man must have an open stance so that he will be able to see the traps and passes develop. He must be ready to rotate to steal the down-court pass, to trap the outside drive past the wing man and to rotate forward whenever the weak side wing man uses a front rotation to try to steal. (Diagram 13-33.)

The middle man also has goal protection responsibilities. He must help control the ball whenever a *dribbler splits inside* between the front three defenders. He cannot rush right at this dribbler *unless* he can stop him immediately. He tries to *contain* him, giving ground, to give the rest of the defense a chance to recover. (Diagram 13-34.) The outside wings hustle to protect their lanes and the point man tries to catch up to trap with the middle man in either case. He must be the top man on the tandem defense with the goalie whenever a team gets a break-through attack in the scoring area. Along this line he will have to cover the goal for 5 to allow 5 to cover the corner at times. (Diagram 13-25.)

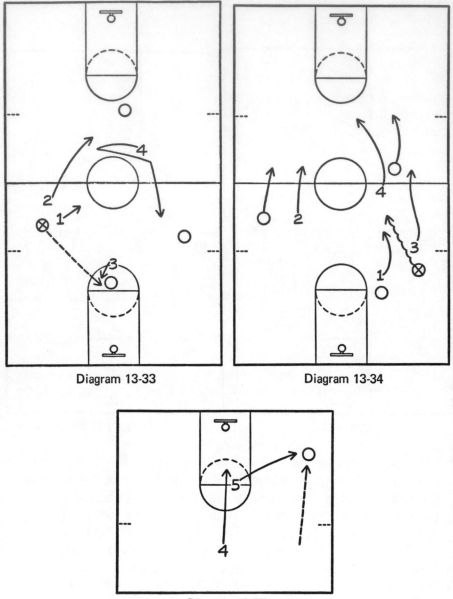

Diagram 13-33   Diagram 13-34

Diagram 13-35

The goalie: The goalie, player 5, will have one paramount job—*prevent the lay-in*. He will *resist every temptation* to leave the goal unprotected. Only when either the middle man or the weak side wing gets back to tell him he is covered can he leave the goal. Five uses the open stance and moves straight back to the goal as he protects it.

A second responsibility touches upon the middle man also.

Some teams will send five players down-court to assist bringing the ball up the floor. When they do, 5 must go up and play tandem with 4. Therefore both 4 and 5 need to know each other's slides. In Diagram 13-36, if the ball comes up 4's side, 5 would move to cover the gaol. If it came down 5's side, he would become the middle man and 4 would get the goal area. This tandem move is vastly important to master. Though need for the tandem happens rather infrequently full court, when this same defense is used at three-quarter or half-court, the tandem move is most necessary. It is expedient for the fourth and fifth men to able to play either middle or goalie.

The Retreat to Half-Court Defense

Many times, more steals will be made by players hustling back into half-court positions than on the initial defensive moves. So often when the ballhandler gets past two or three defenders he relaxes and will lob a pass to an apparently open man only to have a beaten player come in from the blind side to pick off the pass. This is a real lift to the defense. At other times the retreating player will be able to deflect a dribble into a teammate's hands or to help form a trap with a teammate who gets the ball stopped. The entire defensive unit must practice a lot at recovering hard. The best defense to fall into at half-court is normally a zone.

It is easy to fall back to regular man-to-man or it is possible to fall to zone areas and pick up man-to-man the first man they can get. Either way a hard recovery is basic to the good defense and must start around the fifteen-foot scoring radius from the goal. (Diagram 13-37.) We call this "building the defense from the

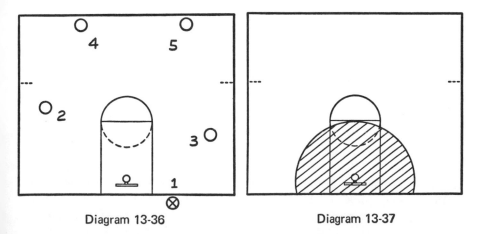

Diagram 13-36   Diagram 13-37

goal." We try to protect the fifteen-foot area first and then play our half-court defense. The main points to remember are to protect the goal first, then stop the ball, and finally protect the scoring areas next to the ball.

Occasions on Which the Middle Trap Might Occur

We try to trap in the outside lanes primarily but at times we will get a middle lane trap. This is fine as long as the team remembers the middle lane trap slides. Diagram 13-38 shows that when a trap occurs in the middle, two men must get to the outside lanes, while the fifth man protects the goal.

In Diagram 13-39 the point-middle trap is shown. We get this trap once in a while. Player 1's rule when the ball is thrown over his head and 4's rule of covering a cutter toward the middle will create this trap.

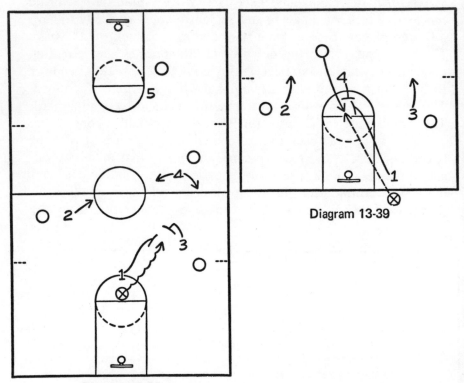

Diagram 13-39

Diagram 13-38

Occasionally a driver will dribble between the front three men and get stopped in the middle, too. This *middle breakthrough recovery* is important to master. The main point to stress here is that the middle man will move up hard to stop the ballhandler if he can get to him immediately. If he feels he cannot stop the ballhandler enabling player 1 to trap with him, he must give ground and back up to help 5 defend the scoring area. Lunging carelessly at the ballhandler will expose the goalie to a three-on-one defensive situation.

Besides the specific drills we have mentioned we find we have a lot of success by working five against five and keeping one team on defense for several possessions. Thus, as soon as it becomes the defensive team's ball, they throw it out of bounds and turn to defend the other end. They play defense at both baskets until it becomes their turn to play offense. The coach can make this competitive by seeing which unit can come up with the best defense out of a certain number of tries in terms of steals and points yielded. Also we have gotten a good bit of mileage out of simply walking through the possible traps and slides without ever running a step. This is especially good for covering an opponent's press offense on the night before a game.

REMINDERS FOR THE MATCHING PRESS

1. Match-up first with their alignment; push the ball to a side; then trap. If they escape, repeat the process.
2. As a player goes to trap he should get his hands up, concentrate on the ball and get between the ball and the man he is leaving so as to deflect a pass or force a lob which may be stolen.
3. Do not let a dribbler split a trap.
4. Do not foul in the traps.
5. Players in the trap must explode back hard just as the ball is passed out of the trap.
6. There are many steals to be gotten by recovering hard when the ball gets past the defense.
7. Never leave the goal unprotected until a teammate yells that he has it covered.
8. On the back rotation the weak side wing man must sprint back toward the goal area hard to help 4 and 5. He will take the goalie position if possible or will move into the middle spot if he cannot release the goalie.
9. A press can be successful even with no steals.
10. The middle man must be sure to adjust back toward the goal gradually as the ball moves toward him. He would move up only to trap or steal.
11. If the weak side wing man who floats the flat pass does not rotate

up to steal and the ball is reversed toward him, he holds on the wing area and lets the point man scramble back to the man he left when he trapped. This keeps a three-man front.

12. Funnel back into the scoring area quickly.

The matching zone press allows the defense to match-up with nearly all offensive alignments. The only times we would not match exactly with the offense would be when we would have to violate the zone principles too much. If a particular move hurts us and we cannot match it up, we can drop our press to three-quarter court or possibly go to the man-to-man, or use a zone press variation described in the following chapter.

14

Adjusting the
Matching Zone Press Defense

Opponents will scout our teams and develop certain moves to combat our zone press as teams must do if they expect to crack any good team's defense. The matching zone is not as vulnerable to scouting as most zone presses, however. This is due to the fact that the matching zone will adjust to the original alignment of the offense. Therefore, the opponent must counter our defense with special cuts or rotations in order to confuse our defenders. We have practiced against many press offenses over the years and have worked out special rotations and adjustments to cover these offenses. Regardless, an opponent will occasionally throw in a new look at us. We expect them to do this. We accept it as a challenge to be able to adjust to their two or three best moves. In general, the offense should run out of moves before the defense is depleted of adjustments.

We have adjusted our defense a number of ways to stop a team which seemed to be going well against our regular press moves. We may make special two or three man rotations to cover the opponent's first move; we may use what we call our "fan" adjustment; we may drop our press back to the three-quarter or half-court line; or we may go man-to-man. Of course, we may simply quit pressing altogether for the moment. But we have found that it is easier for the defense to make adjustments than it is for the offense. The real key is to be able to stay with a defense as long as it is effective and to adjust when the opponent gets timed in against the defense. We do not change just for the sake of change, normally.

SPECIAL ROTATIONS

The following moves are among the zone press offenses that opponents have used against our matching zone press. Any of these moves could have been handled by making our regular moves exceptionally well. But it has been our experience that plays on the floor and on paper do not always work out the same. Therefore, we have found that adjustments to meet the opponent's strength have helped us more than telling our players to "try harder."

After players know the press basics of trapping, floating the press areas, rotating and keeping a three-man front and setting the triangle to back up the trap, they can make any zone or man-to-man press adjustment. The pressure is put on the offense to find a new move.

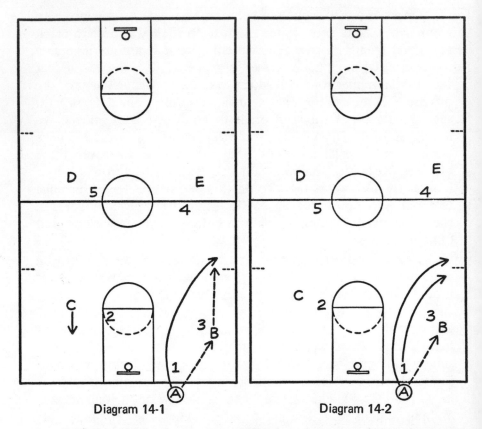

Diagram 14-1   Diagram 14-2

Diagram 14-1 shows one offensive move we have encountered. If players 1 and 3 trap the ball and 2 floats the flat pass, the offense makes 4 cover two men. He may be able to do this if we trap quite well. But when this move hurts us, we tell our players to match-up and stay with their first move, to have the point and wing to rotate. To do this player 1 goes with the cutter, A, to the wing area. (Diagram 14-2.) This makes former wing man 3 the point man now. At this point the press begins and we try to push the ball to a side and trap. It is important that the defense rotate only far enough to cover the move; the point man must not follow the man all over the court. We need a three-man front. He only rotates to the wing and begins zone pressing there.

Diagrams 14-3 and 14-4 show a variation of this offensive move and how the opposite wing man and the point man must rotate to cover. In this situation the opposite offensive wing man cuts quickly behind the man who receives the throw-in. Player 2 rotates with him while 1 stays with player A. Player 3 is now the point man on the ball.

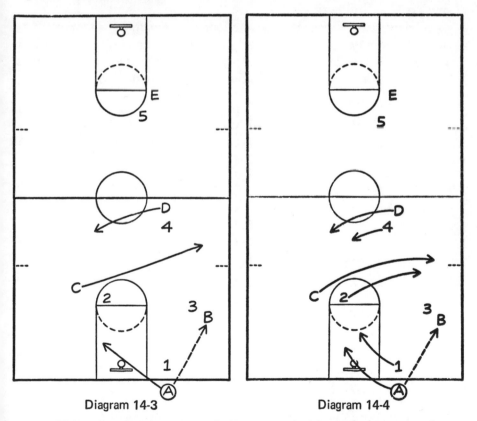

Diagram 14-3   Diagram 14-4

This adjustment accomplishes several things. It prevents the offense from capitalizing on their preferred move. It takes up a few of the ten seconds they have to cross the mid-court line. And it reduces the actual court area we must defend. If player 2 in

Diagram 14-4 traps with 3 against ballhandler B, he can lob over the trap to the man 2 leaves, player C. But 4 has less floor area to cover now and the offense has less space in which to get free. Both are plus factors for the defense.

Diagram 14-5 shows another offensive maneuver. Player D breaks deep up the middle. If 4 covers him, C cuts quickly back and beats 2. If 2 covers D he leaves C open. Either way A gets open usually breaking up the left side. We use a rotation here involving three men. Our point man must rotate with his man to the wing and players 2 and 4 stay with their men's first move. As it ends up in Diagram 14-6 the middle man is on the point, the point is on the wing, and the wing is playing the middle. Again, we are ready to begin pressing. Their best cuts have only gotten the ball in-bounds for them and we intended to allow this to happen anyway. All we have to do is try to push the ball to a side, trap and possibly rotate to steal.

Most moves can be adjusted to in a similar manner. It amounts simply to matching their first cuts on a man-to-man basis. But we will not go man-to-man to the point that they destroy our three-man front plus a back-up man. We want to stay zone.

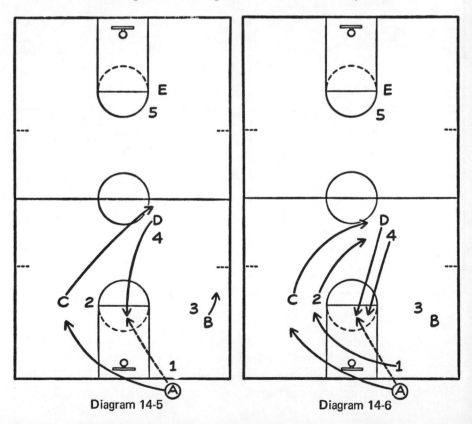

Diagram 14-5   Diagram 14-6

To make the point clear Diagrams 14-7 and 14-8 illustrate two more ways we have adjusted to other moves. Each coach can devise his own adjustments easily enough once he knows the principles of pressing. In Diagram 14-7 the offense is 2—1—2 and the middle man C pulls 2 out of his normal position. To allow him to go will give him an easy pass. So we rotate the point man to 2's wing in order to keep a three-man front. In Diagram 14-8 the offense is 2—2—1 and is all set to give a return pass to A if players 1 and 3 trap. Instead we match the first move by letting 1 stay with A for four or five steps and then we begin our press. We have only a two-man front momentarily, but whichever direction the ball goes will bring the third man, either 2 or 4, into the play.

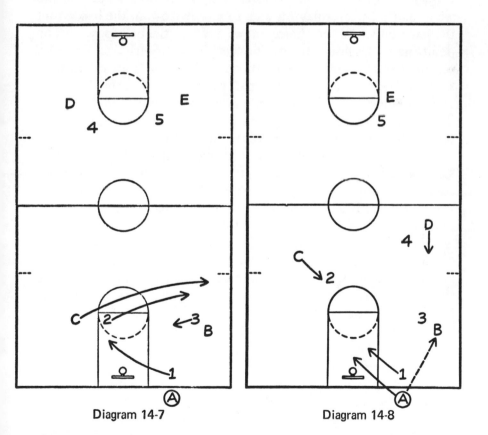

Diagram 14-7   Diagram 14-8

While these adjustments may seem complicated at first, they amount to simply staying matched man-to-man on your man's first cut by rotating from one press position to another. The press will begin as normal after the pass-in.

THE FAN ADJUSTMENT

Going to the fan adjustment has given our press a strange look to the offense without causing our defenders too much of a burden. To distinguish between the two moves, our normal press is a "funnel" move. That is, we attempt to cover the ball with a wing man and trap with the point man. We are in effect funneling the ballhandler into a trap between our front-line defenders. (Diagram 14-9.) The defense may hold positions as the ball is trapped or they may choose to rotate either to the front or back in order to steal.

The fan move is one that *can* happen as part of the regular funnel defense. But when we call for this option we try to make it happen. It involves trying to *force* a back rotation. To do this the wing man must overplay his area so heavily toward the inside that the ballhandler has no choice but to advance the ball forward. The point man does not trap with the wing; he drops back to prevent a return pass in-bounds and to shut off the middle area. (Diagram 14-10.) The idea is to fan the ball to the outside lane. The wing man, 3, stays at the ballhandler's side and encourages a drive right down the outside lane. He stays close enough to prevent the ballhandler from escaping and crossing into the middle lane. The middle man times himself so as to spring a trap on the ballhandler, starting the back rotation. Player 5 moves up to cover the down pass if 2 moves well enough to release 5 from goal coverage responsibility. If 2 cannot make the long slide to the goal, he will move over to cover the down pass for 4.

The fan move makes a good change of pace. It can be overused, but it is effective when a team has had success passing into the middle because this move jams up the middle and forces the ball outside more easily than in the regular move. The middle man, 4, is the key to the success of this adjustment. He must drop back as the ball progresses up the floor but move up to set the trap at the "right moment." The right moment is either at the half-line, or when the dribbler is going fast with the wing man at his side making it difficult to control his body. The middle man must approach the ballhandler with his hands up and in the pass lane to his man so as to force a high pass if the ballhandler elects to throw down-court. The weak side wing man must hustle on the entire move. He must anticipate his long slide and be moving down-court as the ball is thrown in opposite him; otherwise the goal area can suffer.

In the fan move we have forced a back rotation. It is the same set of slides we use when a back rotation comes about under normal conditions discussed earlier. A point to remember is that the fan move is only a first move option. If the ball is reversed or if our defense is broken up some way, we try to form our three-man front and play normal, or "funnel," press defense. That is, if the fan is beaten or fails to materialize correctly, we will resume pressing as in our regular approach.

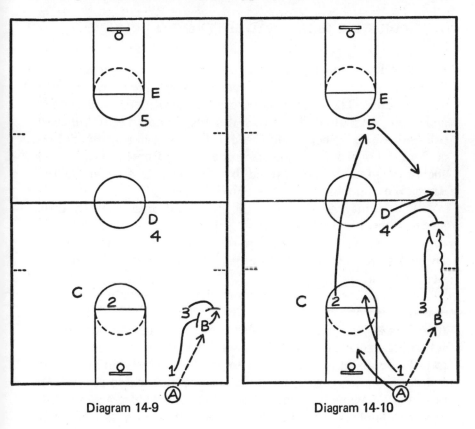

Diagram 14-9   Diagram 14-10

We have used these various options to great success. Although our boys are using the same principles in each case, they cause the offense to have to attack differently. At the first of the year a team may learn only the basic press. Soon they may learn to fan for a while and then funnel for a while as the coach directs or on a special signal. Eventually we have been able to key off the wing men. If the wing is overplaying far inside, this keys the fan move. The point will see this and fall straight back instead of going to the ball. The middle man will be ready to trap as the ball advances. He must learn the timing as to when to leave his man and throw the trap. The weak side wing will fall back toward the middle and observe the goalie. If the goalie is coming up to the middle, the weak side wing will go to the goal. If the goalie is staying, the weak side wing will stay in the middle. In keying this way, which can be done only after the team has matured in the press, the defense can really confuse the offense and prevent them from gaining offensive rhythm.

ADJUSTING THE PRESS TO DIFFERENT COURT LEVELS

We have found that moving our initial point of pressure from full court, the A level, to *three-quarters court,* the B level, is often very effective. The change alone causes the offense to adjust a bit and if they hesitate in doing this, it helps the defense. At times the offense will be quicker than the defense and can beat the defense at the full-court area. A change in the point of pressure can reduce the floor space to be covered by the defense and negate to a degree the opponent's advantage in quickness.

The beauty of adjusting the matching press back to three-quarters court is that the defense makes use of the same slides that they learned for the full court press. The slides, rotations, and principles are the same. The defense will still match-up, push to a side lane, and trap.

There are two points that defenders must keep in mind to be effective in pressing less than full court. The first difference regards matching up. It is not as neat a match-up as when pressing full court. In Diagram 14-11 player 1 is matched up with the man out of bounds but does not get up on him as he would if he were full court pressing, of course. Players 2 and 3 match-up with the next two players but one of them, 3 in our diagram, must be loosely matched with the man who will receive the throw-in, player B. Player 2 has C and 4 takes D. Thus, for a time 1 and 3 are matched up so loosely that they are not even near their men. But all men must get matched up like this or the press will fail. The second difference is in the timing of the press. The actual pressure does not begin until one of the defenders makes "defensive ball contact." This term means that players begin to tighten up and prepare to push the ball to a side and trap when one defender comes within defending range (six feet) of the ballhandler. This ball contact will be made normally by one of the men matched with the two men bringing the ball up the floor.

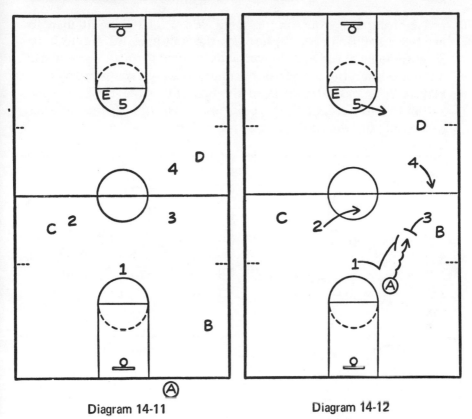

Diagram 14-11   Diagram 14-12

In Diagram 14-12 point man 1 made ball contact and as the dribbler stopped, 3 trapped in the outside lane. Players 2, 4, and 5 adjust to pick up the pass. The press began when 1 met ballhandler A. In Diagram 14-13 the press begins as 3 makes contact with ballhandler B. Player 1 traps with 3 and players 2, 4, and 5 adjust for the pass. Again, if the ball escapes the trap successfully, the defense would try to re-set their three-man front, match-up and push it to a side for another trap. Front and back rotations are the same as always but will employ all five men in rotating more often since help is more available to the goalie because less area is being defended.

Pressing with the match-up at *half-court* has been our best defense in desperate situations. We line up our players in 1–2–1–1 formations as in Diagram 14-14. Point man 1 begins the defensive pressure by making ball contact. The timing of the press will vary once again from pressing either full or three-quarters-court. We worry less about the match-up alignment at half-court and concentrate more on trapping. We want the point man to meet the ballhandler as he crosses the half-line. We try to keep from trapping in the middle lane since it would stretch our defense quite a bit and the ballhandler is under 5-second pressure anyway. Players 2, 3, and 4 try to keep the ball out of the middle. As the ball moves to a side lane the point and wing trap. If the ball goes to a corner the wing and 4, or possibly 5, trap.

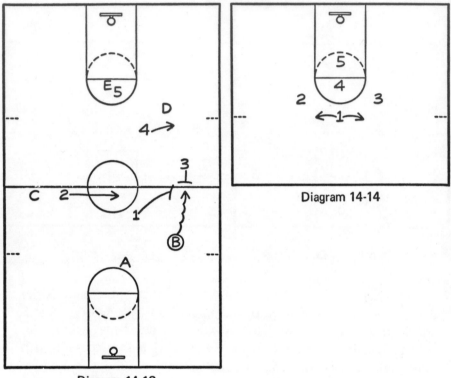

Diagram 14-13

Diagram 14-14

Diagram 14-15 shows player 1 meeting the ball and trapping with 3 on the side. Note that 1 gets in the pass lane back to his man as he traps. He is less concerned about a split than he is a quick return pass since teams are generally trying to slow the game down more than to score when we use this defense. Players 2 and 4 float the pass lanes as 5 stops the goal area. In Diagram 14-16 the ball goes down to the corner where 3 and 4 set a trap. There are two important points to stress with this diagram. One, player 4 must not cover any corner until *after* the ball is thrown or dribbled there. If he tries to get there to steal the pass from B to C, he will open up the vital inside area. Furthermore, he will tend to prevent passes from going to the corner if he shuts off that pass lane; we *want* the ball to go into the corners. Two, the weak side wing man, player 2, *must* cover the high post area as 4 pulls out to the corner. This is the regular move for back rotations it will be recalled, and it is suicide at half-court to miss this slide.

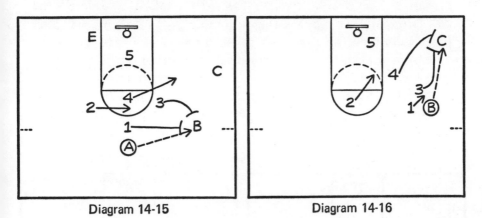

| Diagram 14-15 | Diagram 14-16 |

The only difference in rotating at half-court as compared with other match-up rotations is that as the ball is reversed back around from side to side the players will be able to get right back to their original positions after each rotation since there is no further down-court movement possible due to the out of bounds line. So in Diagram 14-16 if the ball is reversed to the other corner, player 2 will become a wing man again rather than staying in the post for 4. The coach will have to decide whether to have 4 cover both corners or only the first corner the ball goes to and let the goalie cover the reverse corner.

The same press is capable of being used at all levels of the court. The defenders need not learn an entire new defense to accomplish this. With knowledge of the variance in timing borne in mind the players can have three defenses in one. Adjusting our press at these three levels has been a terrific tool for our teams.

OTHER ZONE PRESS VARIATIONS

The coach may decide to use a set formation to begin pressing rather than matching up. He may use full, three-quarters or half-court presses employing the same press principles already discussed. We will briefly examine some of the standard press formations to illustrate how the knowledge of press fundamentals allows a team to press in any zone formation the coach desires.

The original alignment in pressing in not nearly as important as many coaches believe.

The 2–2–1 Press

Diagram 14-17 shows the beginning 2–2–1 alignment. This press will allow the first pass to be thrown in-bounds. Then the defense will push the ball either inside or outside. The overplay to turn the ball inside for the middle lane trap with 1 and 2 is used more often. Keep in mind that the players may be adjusted more or less wide, further up or back, and should adjust somewhat as to how the offense lines up even though they are not matching up exactly.

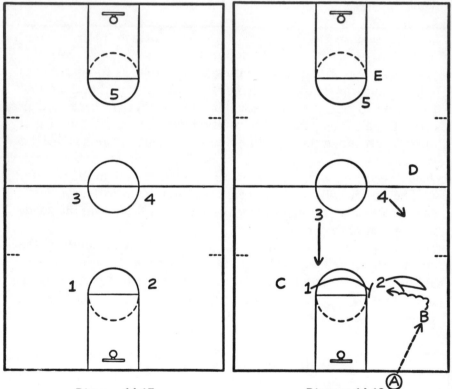

Diagram 14-17   Diagram 14-18

Diagram 14-18 shows the front men turning the ball inside. Players 1 and 2 trap the inside lane so 3 and 4 float the outside lanes as 5 covers the goal. Player 3 has the choice to rotate up to steal a pass to A or to hold and float the area between B, C, and A. Player 4 will get into a back rotation if the pass is thrown to D or if the dribbler gets past 2 and 4 is able to get to him in time to trap with 2. On the front rotation as 3 moves up and the ball is reversed, 4 would move to 3's area and 2 would rotate into 4's spot. In the back rotation 5 would move up to cover for 4 if 3 can get back to cover the goal. Otherwise, 3 would have to move over to cover that down-pass lane.

Diagram 14-19 shows the front men playing closer together and fanning the ball into the outside lane for a trap. The normal move would be for the front man and middle man to trap as shown; however, 1 and 2 could trap in the outside lane, making 3 and 4 the floaters. In our diagram the former option occurs. This is a back rotation. Players 2 and 4 trap and the back-up triangle is set as 1 and 4 float the two pass lanes and the other middle man covers the goal. Again if 3 is slow or asleep, 5 cannot get that pass lane. He must see the help coming before he abandons the goal. Notice how 4 dropped back as the ball travelled up-court to prevent any easy pass and jumped into the trap at a time he felt opportune.

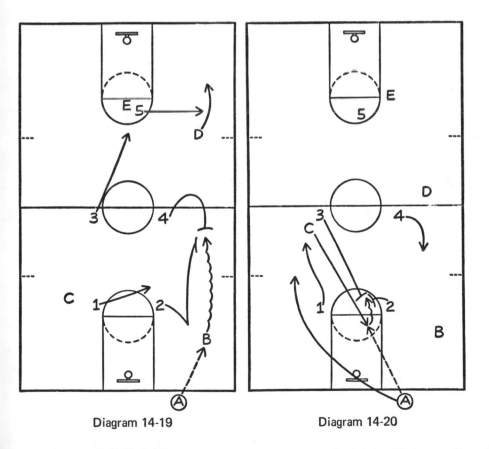

Diagram 14-19   Diagram 14-20

The middle men, 3 and 4, will have to tandem to defend cutters into the middle area for receiving passes. If the ball is thrown into the middle, the nearest middle man will try to contain the ballhandler until a front man can trap with him. Player 2 would trap with 3 and player 1 would trap with 4. This allows proper coverage of the two outside float areas. (Diagram 14-20.)

In summary if the front men get a trap, 3 and 4 must float to steal the pass. When one of the front men pushes the ball outside, the ball side middle man will try to trap with him. If the two middle men trap with each other, the two front men drop back rapidly to float the two pass lanes. As can be observed, the traps will occur in either the middle or outside lanes as in any press. Standard pass lane coverage is used to cover the possible escape passes. The defenders may rotate to steal or hold positions as the situation dictates. Either way the defense will try to re-set after a trap is beaten. Traps set after the initial one will usually be set easier by pushing the ball outside. Once the ball gets beyond the mid-court press area the team may fall back to any defense prescribed by the coach.

The 2–1–2 Press

We will illustrate one more formation for emphasis. It should be clear by now that pressing man-to-man or in any zone formation requires the same basic principles, so the discussion here will be brief. Diagram 14-21 shows the original set-up, but these positions are adjustable. Diagram 14-22 has the defense pushing the ball outside where 2 and 3 set a trap, while 1 and 5 float the pass lanes. Players 4 and 5 are partners who must talk and work tandem with each other. The middle lane trap is set in Diagram 14-23. In general to handle the middle lane trap 3 will elect to cover one float area and the back men can both float. But if the ball escapes, the back man opposite the ball must hurry to cover the basket. Players 4 and 5 can take some chances but must be sure that one of them is aware to cover the goal in each situation.

If the ball escapes a trap and is reversed the defense will try to re-group and trap again. In rotating to the front the coach may allow all five players to rotate as in Diagram 14-24 or may allow only the three front men to rotate as in Diagram 14-25. Diagram 14-26 shows a possible back rotation, but 4 could not get into the rotation unless 1 covers the goal for him. The 2–1–2 is a more effective press at the mid-court area than at full court because players 4 and 5 will not have to get involved in complete rotations when pressing in the smaller area. Three quick men and two big men can run this very well at half-court, especially if the big men work together.

The vital point in our analyses of man-to-man and zone pressing is that the fundamentals of pressing are the same for all presses and that a team can be multiple in its presses if it learns how to press correctly in the first place. A team that can trap, float the pass lanes and rotate can use the same moves with either type of defense and at various court levels.

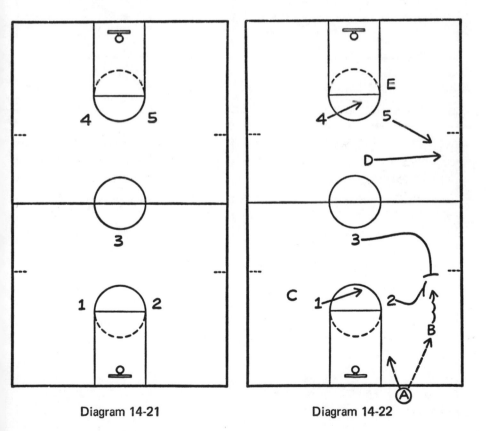

Diagram 14-21   Diagram 14-22

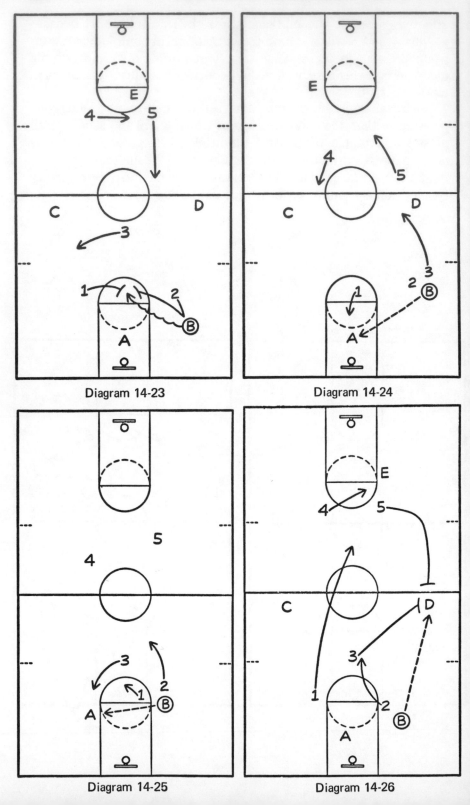

Diagram 14-23

Diagram 14-24

Diagram 14-25

Diagram 14-26

15

Drills for Teaching
Pressing Defenses

1. Full Court One-on-One Offense and Defense

Emphasize turning the ballhandler.

2. Full Court Two-on-Two, Three-on-Three, and Four-on-Four Offense and Defense

Good for conditioning and for defensive habits.

3. First Pass Pressure

Use three-on-three and guard the man out of bounds as well as the two men in-bounds. Try to force a five-second call. Use two or three groups simultaneously.

4. Two-on-One Trap Work

Give one man the ball and keep the two defenders fifteen feet away to start. The ballhandler tries to advance the ball against the two defenders full court. Insist on executing the trap well. If they can stop the man three times, the drill is over.

5. One-on-One Catch-up Drill

Give the dribbler a head start and work the defense to catch-up and cut off the ballhandler. (Full court)

6. Four-on-Two Trap Drill at Full Court

Players 1 and 2 drive the ball forward. As 1 drives against 3 and 4, player 2 drops back to receive a pass from 1 when he is trapped. Players 5 and 6 float the middle area as if they were the weak side floater. They can rotate up to steal if 1 is trapped well or may hold if he is not. Regardless, they allow 2 to get the ball and they force a trap on him while 3 and 4 float. Player 1 moves back to get the ball again from 2. Three traps to each side ends the drill. Players *must* drop hard and fast from the trap when the ball escapes their trap. (Diagrams 15-1 and 15-2.)

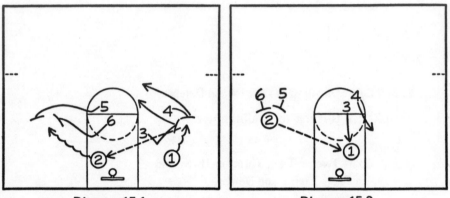

Diagram 15-1   Diagram 15-2

7. Work Four-on-Three and Then Four-on-Four

Have the play end at the half-line. Separate the items to drill on. Work on outside lane traps right and left and then inside lane traps. Drill *holding position* and *rotations* front and back separately. As the season progresses the players can drill this on a whatever-comes-up basis. (Diagrams 15-3 and 15-4.) Do this with both zone and man-to-man. The moves are the same, only the keys to trap differ.

8. Rotations

a. Drill the rotations one at a time. First use four-on-three, then four-on-four just to the half-line. Then work five-on-five but call out the moves to be made and repeat them several times. It is helpful to walk through them at times.

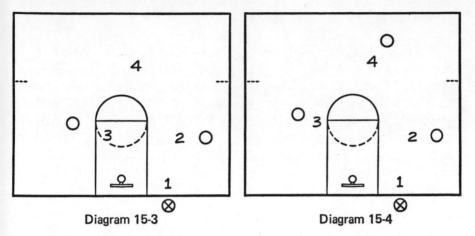

Diagram 15-3   Diagram 15-4

9. Retreat drill.

a. Set up a trap at three-quarters court. Allow the pass to be made successfully down-court about twenty or thirty feet. Make the defenders hustle back, funneling into the fifteen foot area and picking up their assignments quickly.

PART FOUR

THEORY OF DEFENSE

16

The Master Coach
Excels at Teaching Defense

The coach should begin early to develop a definite theory toward the style of game he can believe in and teach best. While it will become necessary to adjust somewhat to each new team and to changes in the game, it is best to keep certain areas of his game intact. One of the advantages of studying the multiple defense game, whether one uses it or not, is that it acquaints the coach with many of the defensive styles available. And regardless of which defense the coach ultimately decides on as his favorite, he must know how each works in order to be able to coach against the various styles. This is one reason we decided to use the multiple defense game. We had to become skilled in playing several types in practice so we could work on beating them in games. Since we got pretty good at executing them, we decided to spend a little more time and incorporate them into our own defensive game.

Coaching at any level has become detailed and complex. Years ago a scouting report might have dismissed the topic of the opposition's defense by describing it simply as man-to-man or zone. A more careful explanation might have included an analysis of the special zone alignment or whether the team switched in its man-to-man. But confronting today's coach are many defenses and countless different ways to play every type. Each causes special problems generally. It is common to hear of teams who possess a dozen defensive variations and who change to nearly that many each game. So subtle have defensive adjustments become that the unwary or ill-advised coach may not even realize his opponent has made a defensive change. Granted, some coaches have the fine athletes who can still win with apparently only one defense. But when the truth is fully known, most of those coaches make occasional appropriate minor adjustments which are just enough to change the offensive pace. In this way the single defense becomes multiple in itself.

This book illustrates various ways to teach the man-to-man, the zone and the press. No team would use all of these defensive variations in any one season. Our teams have at least experimented at one time or another with each defense discussed. We were able to succeed at both the high school and college levels with the same methods of teaching. One of the great coaching fallacies is that boys at lower levels cannot absorb what the college boys can. A good teacher can teach the same things at either level; the subject is not so difficult that it takes a college mentality to handle it. Anything that can be broken into drills can be learned. This book describes how we have undertaken the teaching task. One last thought on this: high school coaches can often teach *more* material to their teams than college coaches because they get a lot more practice time per day than most college men.

Certainly one must be aware at all times of the possibility of overcoaching. But it is our feeling that overcoaching is more apt to occur with the offense than the defense. The coach who gives his team too much offense may confuse his forces. Players can lose the all-important first step because they are unsure or are forced to think too much about their proper cut. Often players become too automatic when they are overburdened offensively. They will fail to capitalize on even the most obvious opening because their moves have been programmed for them in such a way as to blind them to good free lance opportunities. Logically it would seem that if players tighten up offensively, this tension would hamper their ballhandling and shooting. Offensive overcoaching will reduce the chances of success in direct proportion to the amount of confusion and tension that results.

We believe that a player is able to absorb more defensive basketball than offensive. If the player becomes pretty automatic defensively, he has probably done a good thing. He is less likely to become confused defensively because the defense must follow the offensive lead to a large degree. Any tension built up in a player on defense should not affect his ballhandling or shooting because he does not have the ball. If anything, defensive tension will tend to make him more alert. Furthermore, since timing is less of a factor in defense it takes less precision in execution and, therefore, less practice time to learn a defense than it does to absorb an offense.

For these reasons we believe it best to keep the offense simple, the defense multiple.

How much time will a coach devote to coaching defense? Although this is a book on defense and our teams—though often highscoring—have been known for their defense, we believe that less time need be spent teaching defense than is generally thought. Offense requires more skills and more precise timing; therefore, it follows that it should require more teaching time. That is, the offensive player must be able to time his screens and cuts to fit into the offense. He must be able to shoot, dribble, and pass the ball. On the other hand the defensive player can learn a few rules to cover all the situations an offense can put him in. This allows us to teach a larger number of defenses than offenses but we still probably spend a little more *time* teaching offense. We delineate by saying we *emphasize* defense more than offense but we spend a little less teaching time on it even with multiple defenses. In truth, the question of which gets more time, offense or defense, is rather academic. Usually there is a boy playing defense for every one playing offense.

If a coach wants to claim he is a defensive specialist and spends nearly all his time on that aspect, that is his affair. But more important than this is whether the man excels at *teaching* defense. While we believe a coach should do his best to master the man-to-man, the zone, and the presses, he will probably teach one of these types better than the other two. This is especially true for the beginning coach. In the multiple defense system the coach can use his weaker defenses as change-of-pace moves for brief moments while he stays basically with his best defense. For this reason a young man should decide on a defense to learn thoroughly first; then he should begin to pick up as much as possible on the other basic defenses. Even if he never uses them, he will be able to attack them better when he understands each one.

DEVELOP A TEAM DEFENSE PSYCHOLOGY

Teams do not become known for their defense by accident; neither is that honor earned overnight. If a team is to become a first-class defensive unit, the coach must be able to develop a psychology within his players which will enable them to do so both from the team and the individual standpoints. The individual defensive psychology was discussed in chapter 2. Right now let us focus on the mental conditioning we use to aid the development of team defense although each coach will have to adapt his own personality to this problem.

Coaches like to teach defense; fans appreciate a strong defensive effort; and players respect a strong defender. But by nature very few players want to *play* defense. From the first time a boy has contact with the game he will be in love with the offensive aspects—shooting, passing, and dribbling. Many times we have driven down the street and seen a boy shooting and dribbling the ball all alone. It would be a notable occasion if we were to see a young boy working on his defense all by himself. Young players learn early that most attention goes to the scorers. Newspapers, radio-TV announcers, parents, and fans do much to perpetuate the glamour of offense. After a game one of the first questions a player hears will invariably be, "How many did you get?" A boy would be quite surprised if he were confronted initially with, "What kind of a defensive game did you have?" The point of all this is, of course, that unlike scoring, defense must be sold.

The imaginative coach will be able to devise methods to help him sell defense to his players. If he fails to do this his team will not develop a good defense. It takes more than ability and knowledge for a team to be tough defensively. All the skill and know-how available will be wasted unless a team possesses a defensive psychology, a hard-nosed approach to stopping the opponent. Sometimes it takes nearly a whole season, but the good team will eventually accept the defensive challenge. The following paragraphs contain some of the methods we have used to sell our teams on defense.

SELLING DEFENSE TO THE TEAM

We tell our players from the start that the key to success lies in our ability to become a determined defensive unit. While we spend more *time* on offense in practice, we place more *emphasis* on defense as mentioned earlier. We will do much more praising or scolding in front of the group for defensive pluses or minuses than we will for the offensive counterparts. We will teach both offense and defense but will talk a lot more about defense, defensive determination, and pride.

We want our players to encourage one another on defense. We want that compliment given every time for a good defensive move. And we as coaches give it, too. Think of the times you have heard a coach say "Nice shot," or "Way to hit that thing," when a player made a basket. What for? Everybody in the gym knew that it was a good shot. It went in the goal! Players need defensive praise; the man who puts one in the basket has already gotten his reward.

We illustrate to our players that consistent winning teams play good defense and that good defense breeds this consistency. The cliché about teams having "off" offensive nights but not defensive ones is basically true. But it is not absolutely true because we have seen teams have poor games on defense due to being either physically or mentally unprepared. So we say that teams who stay very *diligent* on defense will have an off night far fewer times than the team that is mainly offense oriented. By doing this we promote both defense and diligence.

We sell our players on the idea that most games are won by what we call the "defensive spurt" or "gap-time." We keep a possession chart that tells us what defense we used at all points in the game and indicates what happened in sequence each time either team gained control of the ball. An example of this chart is in chapter 1. By studying the chart we have concluded that teams play most of the game on even terms. But each team will normally have two, three, or possibly more offensive lapses. They will have the ball five or more consecutive times without scoring during each of these dry spells. We call this the "defensive spurt" because we credit the defense with causing this, whether it always does in actuality or not. It usually does. The team able to inflict more "defensive spurts" against the opponent will most often be the winner. During the defensive spurt the team causing it must be able to convert points at their own end of the floor. We call this "gap-time." The team that wins the game is usually able to outscore its losing opponent in a gap-time by a significant margin at least once more during the game than the opponent does to them. When players understand this principle, they gain a little extra respect for the value of defense.

It is difficult to get players to play rugged defense the entire game. Even the most dedicated athletes will not be able to shut out the opponent very long. Good offense is simply superior to good defense. It takes a great defensive effort to stop good offense. Still we try to get the most defensively out of our players at all times. We take tired or ineffective defenders out of the game; we bench poor defenders; we even embarrass them at times. But, being realistic we feel we get a little extra at times from our players by emphasizing the gap-time. When we want to pull away from a team and break a game open, we call for gap-time, or our players may feel some defensive momentum at times and call for gap-time among themselves. During this defensive spurt they will really dig in on defense. Each man will make a supreme effort to stop the opponent. On offense, they will go for the good two-pointer. They will try to outscore the opponent 8 to 1 or 10 to 2, etc., during this period of time. If we can force the opponent to take a time out our boys come to the huddle really fired up. If we fail to pull off the *coup,* nothing is really lost by having played our toughest defense. We will try it again later either way. In fact we admit that we may not always stop the offense; it is a percentage game like all the rest of basketball.

What we have done is to take a positive psychological approach toward defense in our attempt to sell it. Many people say games are won because one team gets "hot" and outscores the loser during a particular period of time. It is all a point of view. For the coach wanting to sell defense to his team it is more appropriate to credit victory to defensive spurts—that time the defense arched its back and withstood the onslaught, allowing their offense to score more than the opponent. What we advocate is the football "goal-line defense" psychology. If inspired footballers can stop the offensive thrust and steal the momentum of the game for their own offense, so can a fired up basketball team.

EXAMPLES OF A WINNING DEFENSE

Following are two pertinent examples of how the defensive spurt won games for us in which we scored 145 and 137 points respectively. While we could point out dozens more it is best to consider these games because the immediate reaction to scores of 145-80 and 137-115 would be to acknowledge some kind of offensive powerhouse. In truth defense set up both wins. Our team was aroused by actions of the opponent the previous year in the first game. For this game our boys wanted to have gap-time early in order to have a really convincing victory. The opponent had been doing well in recent games and we were away from home, so we wanted a good start. After two and one half minutes we were ahead 16-2. The game was over. We played no one more than twenty-two minutes the entire game and our devastating gap right at the start set the stage for a runaway. In the 137-115 game we were on the road again, this time for a tough conference game. We had not won on that floor in twenty years. With three minutes to go in the first half we were tied 46-46. We went into a determined press bid from a time out. In the next three minutes we scored sixteen points; they failed to score at all. Most of the rest of the game was played even. It ended 137-115 so the defensive effort which provided the gap was the key to victory.

The fact that we believe that these defensive spurts win games does not give a boy a reason to coast at other times during the game. We always let our players know when they have been taken out for poor defense. We tell them that they must hustle in games and practices on the defense and rebounding in order to play. We say that the player who depends on his shooting to keep him in the game better be sure he is always having a very hot night because it takes a tremendous lot of offense to keep a boy in the game who does not do well on defense and loose balls.

The coach can help himself in selling hard defense to particularly offense-minded players by pointing out how it often sets up the offense. The boy who plays a forcing defense will get more steals. The opponent will make more mistakes, giving the ball back over more often. The good strong defense is really the offense's best friend. In a year in which our team averaged over 100 points per game, we firmly believed our defense was primarily responsible. Players can see when their good defense has set up their offense.

All in all it is not too hard to sell players to play hard team defense, as long as the coach remembers that it must be sold. A little effort here and there will go a long way. We have our players vote on the top defensive player each year and we give him a nice trophy at our awards banquet. Aside from daily praise from the players and coaches, we make sure the communications media recognize players for their good defense. We sell defense through our radio and newspaper interviews and club talks to fans and parents. If we can get them to become more aware of the importance we are placing on defense, then they can join our sales crew and help reinforce what we are telling our players. Defense can be sold.

The coach will know when the team has bought the defensive idea. Players will feel a twinge of pain, a loss of pride, when a man scores in his area. The team will talk *on* defense and they will also talk defense. The players with lesser ability will come along faster when playing for a defensive-minded team. The boys with less talent can find defensive roles in games. Overall spirit will improve because each man can feel important as a part of the good team defense whether he is a big scorer or not. We have never known a really rugged defensive team that lacked *esprit de corps.* Strong team defense builds good team spirit.

SELLING MULTIPLE DEFENSE TO THE TEAM

Selling *multiple defense* is easy once the team accepts the challenge to become tough defensively. The coach can explain that since the opponents will be using a variety of defenses over the season, the team must practice against several possible defensive styles. Since it is of little help to practice against a poorly-executed defense, the team should learn to perform the defenses well. If, indeed, they learn to do several defenses well, they might as well use them in a game as occasions demand. Furthermore, a change of defense is often what sets the stage for a defensive spurt. The team with no defenses to change up with must rely solely on determination and luck.

What the coach has done when he sells defense to his team is to put their thinking in line with what he knows they must do to win. He will have made each boy aware of the importance of team defense. The team will have accepted a defensive psychology. When this is accomplished each player will be receptive to the more special mental approach he must possess to make him a tough individual defender within the framework of the team defense. These things will never happen on a team unless they are made to happen. We refer to it as forming a defensive psychology because what is observed during the game must come from within; from players whose minds have been prepared for the big defensive effort.

SETTING UP THE LEARNING SITUATION

Selling defense to the players is a big hurdle to clear; it sets the stage for the next problem, *teaching* it. Players psychologically ready for defense have an easier time learning it but the coach must still be adept at teaching in order to build the best defense. Although the coach will be anxious to get his defense into operation, we recommend that he teach offense first and start his sales campaign on defense at the same time. He may teach one-, two- and three-man defensive drills right away, but not team defense. If he concentrates on teaching team defense before the team learns the offense, he will discourage the players on offense and make them doubt the worth of the coach's offense. Any offense takes a lot of time to teach. The players should spend at least their first seven practices almost entirely on offense. Players already know some defense anyway but they must be taught to run a five-man offense. If a coach works backward and teaches team defense first, his team will have a lot of trouble gaining offensive confidence and poise. Besides, it will put the defense to a better test to run it against a team that can execute some offensive moves fairly well. When the coach feels the offense is getting somewhat secure he can begin working the team defense into practice.

It is equally important to build confidence in the team defense, but teaching offense first will not hamper this if the coach explains what he is doing. In fact, teaching the offense first will help prepare the players for defense. It is most difficult for a player to stay in the proper defensive position unless he is in good physical condition. At the beginning of the season, players seldom have themselves in the necessary kind of shape it takes to play half of a game in a defensive stance. After working a week or so the players are more prepared to begin concentrated defensive work. Breaking the defensive material slowly to the players will help breed confidence, also. The coach should have players make defensive moves against imaginary offensive players and then against half-speed offensive men before letting the defense face live offense. Recall that we believe it takes less time to teach defense than it does offense so the coach can afford to break it down and teach it well.

Some eastern coaches have been teaching a style of defense that is predicated on the idea that the defense can "deny" the ball from his opponent. Some of these coaches have done quite well and are outstanding coaches. Hovever, we believe the term, "deny," is not appropriate to building defensive confidence. It is impossible for a player to deny the ball from his opponent, absolutely, even within a particular area. He can certainly give his man fits but we fear that a boy will get discouraged too often if we insist on denial, knowing it cannot be attained. It may be a small thing but we ask our players to do most of these same defensive moves without referring to it as absolute denial. Our basic defensive strategy is to force the offense to do something they do not want to do and to make them function under the worst possible conditions. We intend to force them out on the floor. We want to disrupt their flow in passing and cutting. We want our players to believe they can do this a great percentage of the time.

HOW TO USE DRILLS IN TEACHING DEFENSE

To teach defense successfully the coach must devise drills which teach exactly what he wants his players to do. Educators point out that in the learning situation the learner will absorb more readily that material which is meaningful and useful. He will also be more favorably disposed toward working at those kinds of tasks. For these reasons it is vastly important that the player see just how each drill will carry over to what he is to do in a game. Most coaches should throw away about half the drills they presently use because they fail to pass this test. Students will be more eager to learn when they can see some results from what they are doing. Proper drilling will produce the desired results. The careless teacher takes quite a risk.

The teacher-coach must make use of the whole-part method of teaching as he instructs his players on defense. He will show the entire team defense to his players at first and at certain later intervals, but will begin his teaching at the individual level. He will teach stance, body position, footwork, and so on. Next, he will put two on two, then three on three. In the two and three man exercises the offense will force the defense to defend against all the basic scoring moves. Alert coaches are always on the watch for drills to help them. There are some fundamental drills that nearly all coaches use and there are some beneficial ones that coaches can learn from their colleagues. This book offers some of the standard drills and a few that are not. It is best to adopt only those drills that teach exactly what the coach wants taught. He should apply himself to devising the necessary drills when he feels an inadequacy in his teaching.

While it is best to use the whole-part methods throughout the season, the early season workouts should emphasize the parts. Once the season is well underway it is best to concentrate more on the whole. There should always be some part work, mainly on particular weaknesses exhibited in the whole defense in games as the season progresses. Most teaching the last two-thirds of the season will be whole teaching. That is, we will concentrate on the individual defense but within the framework of the five-man team defense.

The coach should remain aware of the use of intervals in teaching. We have wasted a lot of time trying to go over and over something we were not doing well. Eventually the players lost their edge and interest while the coaches lost their patience. We have learned to say that we cannot master everything in one day.

It is wise to drop a ragged effort and come back to it a few minutes later, at the end of practice or the next day. Far better learning will occur this way.

Coaches should not neglect teaching the full court aspects of the game of basketball. A lot of instructing may be done at half-court but the game is played full court. If the coach never teaches full court, he will be disappointed as he watches his team perform poorly in games. To accomplish this we use several devices. Scrimmage is the most obvious one. On other occasions we will make one team be the defense all the time. As soon as they gain possession they turn it over to the other team out of bounds and play more defense on the other end. We also use two groups of five to alternate playing against one team. After each dead ball the two teams alternate who are playing against the one. We can use the defensive teams as the alternating ones and have them change defenses each time they go back in the game. This also helps teach the offensive team how to adjust to defensive changes. We try to use the score clock in practice quite often, too, because the game is played with it on. Another device we use is one we adopted from football. We designate certain days to teach offense and others to teach defense once we get past the first couple of weeks of practice.

Basically, the coach's task is the same as that of any other teacher. He must keep a good classroom atmosphere to teach well. He must regard the emotional climate, the gym temperature, the physical strength left in his players, the length of their attention span, and their overall attitude. He must learn how to teach best what he feels he ought to teach. Once he has his players sold on the value of the lessons he is teaching he should be able to apply sound teaching principles to transfer his knowledge to their abilities. The coach's final concern will be to keep his players motivated. Motivation is the basic problem for every teacher. The coach being no exception, he must constantly seek new ways to spur his players. Through his own hard work and enthusiasm he will have to lead them through the learning plateaus to greater peaks. Therefore, the coach never can relax on his teaching. It is the difference between the average coach and the master coach.

TEAMMANSHIP

We have coined the term "teammanship" in order to express what we expect from our team members. Teammanship can mean whatever the coach wants it to but we believe it is a term that says a lot in itself to players without too much elaboration at first. As a season progresses the concept can be developed to inculcate all those positive aspects the coach feels his program should possess. To us it has meant every man doing his part to build a terrific team attitude. By doing this we have had the good fortune to go through an entire season without any fights or arguments between any two players and without anyone making a single complaint to the coaching staff. It may sound unbelievable, but it is quite true nonetheless.

In order to accomplish teammanship with our players we do the best we can to promote things we believe will develop it. We are not master psychologists and certainly do not know every patent answer but we do what we think best. We start by talking about teammanship the very first day. We issue a player's handbook that does not have a single play in it. Its approximate thirty-page length contains ideas. It has our concept of team attitude written on the very first page. If much of it reads as if Norman Vincent Peale could have written it, it is by all means intentional. We want our players to learn to concentrate on positive aspects. They should learn to think in terms of success, of actualizing a goal. They must develop a winning attitude and come to realize that this, coupled with great effort, will lead to the improvement it takes to know victory in the broadest sense.

The player handbook also sets forth our ideas about training rules, practice discipline, offensive theory, defensive theory, and some helpful hints on the fundamentals of the game. But there are no plays because we teach offense and defense in other ways. We want our players to know our thinking behind the whole program first. Then the things we do will make more sense to them. They will work intelligently and diligently when they can see how the effort fits into the overall setup.

We ask our players to write out and hand in a paper realistically expressing their team and individual goals for that year. We lead the players to what we think might be good general guidelines, but have learned to avoid influencing the goals too much. One season we would have settled for a conference championship and an approximate 20-8 record. But a transfer player taught us a lesson about our own concept of positive thinking leading to goal fulfillment. We had won our first five games before dropping one. When someone mentioned how we could still get about twenty wins, he let everyone know we could still win all but one game, the one we had just lost. And through his continuing contagious efforts we won the next nineteen in a row. This does not happen in every instance, but do not deride your boys for shooting for the moon, if they realize the work it takes to hit it. At any rate it is very important to agree on two or three things to accomplish that year. Then keep talking about it, make it a real thing, Hold that image in front of your team. Even write it on a sign. Do not allow them to forget. Try to select only two or three things—possibly two minor items and one major target. It is important that one goal not be consummated until the end of the year. It is bad to have goals that are reached too early or that are out of sight too soon. If a mistake occurs on this, call a meeting during the season and set a new goal. Your team must be directed toward the desired prize to maintain determination over the year. I remember our setting a goal at being .500 percentage-wise my first year in college coaching. This was a big aim with a team who had won two games the year before. But when we won enough games that .500 was guaranteed, we still had several games remaining on our schedule. We had aimed too short. This is why we say not to induce your boys to shoot too low. Let youth's enthusiasm become yours. As you preach believing, it is nice to develop some of the quality yourself. By your students you are taught.

HOW TO USE TRAINING RULES

Our approach to training rules is not unique but it is worth mentioning because it relates to teammanship. We believe in applying as few rules as possible. People who have teammanship in mind will not do things which will hurt their play. They have team pride so that they try hard to avoid doing things that would bring embarrassment to our team. At times we have had players draw up their own short list of rules; in other years we have had no formal rules at all. A useful piece of advice here though is to keep track of the number of practices your team has remaining as the season draws to an end. It is surprising how many calendar days are actually left when there are only twenty practices left in the season. When it gets down to twenty, or whatever number one would select, the coach should inform his team. Then he can ask for a concentrated effort on the self-discipline it takes to prepare for tournament play. Since he has made few demands on this line all year, the boys will usually respect his desire. After all, there are only twenty practices left and it will be over. But in those six or seven weeks a dedicated team can peak into top shape for tournament play, and do it willingly. This approach helps avoid the staleness five months of "hounding" about training can cause.

We operate our practices with the purpose of developing attitudes as much as skills. The players vote at the end of the year for the "Most Inspirational Player." This boy will get a trophy and we make it a good one. We want that bit of hardware to be premium material. The inspirational player is one who encourages another player daily in different ways to do the best he can do. He brings out the best in another. To facilitate this we insist that players tell another "thanks" in some way—a nod, a hand-slap, a word—for an assist. We want players on either team in a practice scrimmage to tell a player about his good offensive or defensive play. We stress heavily the importance of encouraging teammates. If some boys are not doing it satisfactorily, we call them in and want to know why. It is most important for the top players to compliment the others. Encouragement from the top means twice what it does from the bottom. The leading players have a big obligation. It is too easy for them to sit back and soak up the plaudits. They must give out more than they receive if the coach is to develop teammanship. The top players will have to be told this, hopefully only once but as often as it takes. This is a pivotal factor.

The coach becomes aware that the team is progressing successfully when players competing for the same spot are battling each other tooth and nail, yet encouraging each other to do better. Yes, at first there may be some artificiality involved. We admit this to our players. Make them do it anyway. Pretty soon they will believe in it. This develops the team friendship and confidence necessary for victory. Confidence in oneself can best be sustained over a period of time when all the players keep the encouragement alive. If we hear a negative comment, we stop and ask just how this statement will help anyone. Our point is usually sustained.

Can a team stay competitive and do the kind of encouraging, positive things mentioned? Some coaches like the cocky, step-on-anybody player. I will be the first to say that I like the fighter-type, too. I want a fiery player, one who has to work to control his emotions. Some of the nicest boys I have had—gentlemen in every way—I would not have wanted to guard me because they were such fierce competitors. We put a terrifically high premium on what we call "gritty determination." It is one of the essential ingredients to winning. Yet we have had few overt conflicts among players because that would violate teammanship.

When the inevitable fight does occur, we get it out in the open and have the apologies forthcoming in a hurry. A fight or argument is no real problem, but lack of forgiveness and understanding are. Tell the boys at the start that conflict may happen and inform them just how to deal with this minor sorespot.

We think we prevent a lot of physical turmoil by the nature of our approach, but just as important is our policy on fouling. In any drill or scrimmage a man who fouls must hold up his hand. Unless it is a really bad one we do not usually stop the play or say anything at all. But the fouled man has lost nothing if the boy who fouled confesses. And the fouling player really has little to lose by owning up to the contact. What makes for trouble is when a boy is fouled and no one says a word. He figures the guilty man has taken unfair advantage of him, that the coach has seen him look bad and he must repay the villain. But the confessed foul exonerates the man fouled from his failure and so everyone feels much better. This must be a team effort though. We had about as much trouble with one boy who simply refused to acknowledge even to himself he was capable of fouling as he went his way through practice crippling people as we would have had without our rule. No amount of talking helped. So he generally gave and got it back until the day he quit the team. We do not win them all either.

Some coaches insist on controlling the group makeup in order to promote team play. A lot of successful men have written how they rotate roommates on trips and travelmates in cars and so on. So we did that for a few years, too. We rotated cars and the whole thing. But it seems now that it is just as well to recognize before the group that the coach wants all the boys to think in terms of the team and the team goal. And being realistic, there will be two or three boys who get along well and will want to be with each other more than with any others. On any team there will be three or four of these small groups. It happens regardless of the coach's group control devices. Therefore, we recognize and condone it. But we advise them that each group must be sensitive to the extent that they must never *exclude* a team member from a group under *any* circumstances. Each group must like and respect another. Each team member must be aware that it is a violation of teammanship to use the group as a wailing wall to criticize another player or the coach. All avenues of communication must be kept open to the understanding but firm coaching staff so that the group is not necessary as a complaint forum. If the groups are *positive* in nature, all will go well.

Many of our points on teammanship will sound idealistic, perhaps superfluous to some. But this is what we teach and boys who adopt our philosophy certainly make excellent boys to coach. We teach the carry-over aspects of basketball playing and teammanship above all. We tell the boys the first day that these are more important than winning, but that they help develop victory. We feel they are even more important than sportsmanship and the man who develops these factors has greater gains. Sportsmanship to most people means shaking hands and smiling after losing. Developing that trait is far secondary to what we have been talking about. Personally, we can understand the bitter loser. The ungracious winner is more perplexing.

In summary, teammanship involves developing those intangible qualities that make a group of boys a team. Once a coach decides what his image of "team" is he can define his own characteristic teammanship.

A BRIEF PHILOSOPHY ON THE GAME

It is important for a coach to have a sound knowledge of the mechanical aspect of the game but it is not as significant in producing a successful career as is his approach toward coaching as a profession. Not all coaches will accept this viewpoint but most experienced coaches reach a point in their lives when this message begins to make sense to them. All the technical knowledge in the world will eventually go to waste if a coach has a poor mental approach to the game and in his personal dealings relative to it. The problem is similar to one we coaches encounter occasionally when working with young players. When given a choice between the boy with fine natural talent whose attitude limits him and the player of lesser ability who is ready to pay every price to make good, most coaches prefer the latter. So it is with coaches—approach overshadows raw talent in the long haul.

This does not mean that one may be a poor student of the game and survive in coaching. Far from it! Part of the successful coach's philosophy will include the importance of staying abreast of the changes in the game. He will always be seeking better ways to teach what he knows in an effort to get things into the simplest communicable form for his players. But too many coaches fail to see that their profession goes far beyond their knowledge of the game. As a beginning coach I used to brush aside the opening chapter or two of coaching books regarding philosophy in my eagerness to get to what I considered to be the "meat" of the book. It did not take me too many bumps and bruises of one kind or another to realize that even if a man knew everything about the game, he might still be a coaching failure. So my advice to all young coaches now is to develop a basic philosophy with open ends to leave a lot of room for additions or alterations. It is the successful man who dwells more on *how* to teach and *how* to fulfill his role as coach than he does on *what* to teach.

It is one thing to set forth certain standards and another to fulfill them at all times. Yet, given human weakness, I would like to share some of the thinking that I have tried to follow. The philosophy one adopts as a coach will depend a great deal on his approach to living as a whole. It would not be good to try to copy exactly another's approach unless it would happen to coincide with what one believes as a person. Regardless, the sharing of ideas is a healthy thing to do.

It is fundamental for a coach to look upon his task as more than playing and winning an intermittent series of games throughout life. Granted, a coach should try to win every time his team plays, but coaching as a profession must mean far more than that or it is a ridiculous waste of life. The coach should view the realm of sports as an aid to developing his players for the larger world of life. He must always be searching for ways in which the game can contribute to one's ability to function in the world. In this way the athletic endeavor can be the kind of educational experience that young men would find nearly impossible to duplicate in any other way. Athletes should have the opportunity to cash in on their experience to the fullest. The coach who concentrates only on winning and losing will hamper his players from gaining the broader experience. He must help them to see more than just the immediate.

The coach is a lab instructor in the basketball laboratory of life. So many things in the game correlate to life that the coach owes it to his players to point out various relevant aspects as situations allow. When one is aware, he can draw out analogies from practice and game occurances that make good teaching points. For example, games are rarely lost because of a poor pass or missed shot. Those are what the fan will recall or what the sportswriter beats out for the morning press. The coach and players are capable of analyzing losses or victories better than that. It is my opinion that mental approach, both individual and team, determines the outcome of most games. The fan points to the mistake, the steal, the rebound, the big play. But what set the stage for these was an invisible attitude best identified by the participants. Attitude and personality factors are always working behind the scenes and the wise coach will be able to spotlight the roles played by these unchartable heroes and villains. Without belaboring the point, I will just mention that such a factor as poise has contributed more to a last minute victory than the twenty-foot jump shot. The fan remembered seeing the shot go in. Poise, or lack of it, often determined which team shot it. The coach should make allusion to these points so that all may strive for possession of that excellent quality, poise. It takes only a little imagination to elaborate on the many possibilities available along this line of thinking.

The coach should assist his players in their response to pressure. So much of life is regulated by decisions which are made under pressure. Those who learn to handle pressure in one area of life, athletics, should be better fitted to respond to it favorably in other phases. Practices offer daily experience with pressure and games are filled with it. Administrators used to decry this element in sports. Yet it can be the finest quality athletics offers, especially when a coach can help his players recognize how to deal with it—win or lose. Players gain confidence in themselves when they beat the pressure, if it be by making a free throw in only a practice scrimmage or before a state finals throng. And one of the beautiful things about it is that even in failure a boy learns a lot. He may see the need for more practice or a more positive approach to tight situations. Regardless, he learns that hit or miss, the sun rises the next day and one success or failure does not mean *everything*.

There are innumerable other correlations to life which we will only mention: sacrificing for a goal, cooperation, loyalty, passing beyond barriers of pain and fatigue, and a mass of other aspects which amount to slices out of life. A person will respond in general the rest of his life the way he reacts on the athletic field. The athlete should be made aware of these points as they arise so he has the proper opportunity to recognize and master these situations. This is the way I have tried to approach the coaching profession. Each man must develop some kind of approach with which he can live and work with justification.

Index